In Lincolnshire Long Ago

by

DOUGLAS LAMMING

HUTTON PRESS
1994

Published by
The Hutton Press Ltd.,
130 Canada Drive, Cherry Burton,
Beverley, East Yorkshire HU17 7SB

Printed and bound by

Clifford Ward & Co. (Bridlington) Ltd.,
55 West Street, Bridlington, East Yorkshire
YO15 3DZ

ISBN 1 872167 60 8

DEDICATION

To the most underrated of counties

CONTENTS

AUTHOR'S NOTE AND ACKNOWLEDGEMENTS

Adapted excerpts from Chapters 6 and 7 and a section of Chapter 10 have appeared in *Lincolnshire Life* entitled "A Sporting Revival", "Tuppenny Matinee" and "Trips to Skeggy, Twenties Style" respectively.

The book is an impression of a small Lincolnshire town, and of growing up there in the 1920s. Any lapses in emphasis or detail are due to that fallible instrument, the human memory.

My thanks go to Mrs. Claire Tomalin, former Literary Editor of the *New Statesman*, and Bridon Fibres & Plastics Ltd., for ready permission to use the two quotations below. I am also indebted to several kind people for assistance with certain illustrations, either by their provision or making old material 'fit to print'. In alphabetical order they are A. L. Anderson, the late Ted Byron, J. Norman Clarke, Brendan Kerney, Grahame Mellanby, Eric Redshaw, David N. Robinson (who also kindly provided the Foreword) and the late Mrs. Alfreda Wyld. My cousin, the late Ken Lamming, showed his usual professional competence in designing the book's colourful cover.

DOUGLAS LAMMING
North Ferriby
1994

Remember those long hazy days, crammed with adventure from dawn to dusk?

Life was wrapped up in an ear of corn, pulling funny faces, or a race to the top of the tree. Fact and fiction overlapped; problems were just for grown-ups ...

BRITISH ROPES advertisement copy, 1973.

Maybe someone who is going to be a writer is more impressionable than those other children among whom he sits, but if so he knows nothing about it at the time ...

ALAN SILLITOE in a book review, December 1974.

BY THE SAME AUTHOR

A Century of English International Football, 1872-1972 (with Morley Farror).
A Who's Who of Hull City AFC, 1904-84 (Hutton Press, 1984).
A Who's Who of Grimsby Town AFC, 1890-1985 (Hutton Press, 1985).
A Scottish Soccer Internationalists' Who's Who, 1872-1986 (Hutton Press, 1987).
Who's Who of Liverpool, 1892-1989 (Breedon Books, 1989).
An English Soccer Internationalists' Who's Who, 1872-1988 (Hutton Press, 1990).

FOREWORD

by David N. Robinson,
Associate Senior Lecturer, University of Nottingham and
former Editor of *Lincolnshire Life*.

I had the good fortune, like Douglas Lamming, to grow up in Horncastle. My memories of the 1930s may be clear, but not as clear or sharply drawn as those of the previous decade that you will find in this book. It might have been a town which had seen better days, but always it seemed homely and friendly.

Experience of schools, both 'little' and 'big', were character forming between the wars, and chapel and Sunday School played a significant part in our lives. Apart from the thrill of the Saturday matinée at the cinema, the Treats and the Galas, we made our own amusements (do you remember playing fag cards?). Then there were the sporting events — football and cricket matches, and the fever which gripped the town each year on the occasion of the Skegness to Horncastle Walk.

Strangely, Douglas and I did not meet until 1980 when he came on a weekend course called 'Getting into Print' which I was running at the Horncastle Residential College, although I felt I knew him well from his contributions to *Lincolnshire Life*. We spent almost as much time reminiscing as talking technicalities, and I was delighted to learn that he had in mind compiling this book.

It is not just nostalgia for days long gone; nor is it just a piece of personal local history. It is an accurate and evocative pen picture of a period which, I suppose, will soon be ancient history to some, and it is eminently readable. You can hardly help but enjoy it.

ONE : LOCALE

When you had climbed the steep hill to the west of the little town the reward was a panoramic view. In the valley below buildings spread in no discernible design. Slate or pantile roofs surmounted mellowed brickwork, occasional white splashes indicating whitewashed walls. Trees obtruded everywhere, singly and in clumps.

Obvious landmarks, even to a native, were few — the broad, squat church tower capped by its small 'candle snuffer' spire, a couple of windmills, a bakery chimney and, if fine, the glint of sun on water where river merged into disused canal. And, parallel to the water, a railway line ran southwards from the station, a terminus. To the north and east beyond the town the land rose steadily and continuously, for here the Wolds began.

At this time, the 1920s, the road from our vantage point was flanked by no building other than an ancient single-storey dwelling halfway down. Over the road's bordering hedge-crowned banks stretched fields, both arable and grass, these last close-cropped by grazing livestock. At the hill foot, though, with the sweeping curve into a house-lined West Street, the feel of open country was dispelled.

"... a small town of Georgian softness" a writer recorded in 1971. Half a century earlier this description would, of course, been even more apt. Few buildings dating from later than 1850 lined the main thoroughfares. The mostly cobbled roads resounded with the noise of horse traffic although motor vehicles were becoming increasingly common. Rumbling coal merchants' and brewers' drays were pulled by powerful shire horses; these horses, too, being used for grain laden wagons whose fronts bore the farmer's name and address in elaborate lettering on brightly painted scrolls. Bakers' vans, milk carts and private traps had fleeter horses or ponies, their hooves making a cheerful staccato clip-clop when cantering.

The triangular shaped Market Place was entirely cobbled except for an asphalted area that housed traders' stalls on Saturdays. A Gothic style memorial to a long dead M.P. occupied its centre, guarded by ornate railings destined to be sacrificed to the nation's scrap iron stocks during World War Two. Three-storey buildings bounded the Market Place, the short High Street running from it. Having three storeys was often the sole similarity between neighbouring properties, there being a hotch-potch of differing heights and contrasting architecture. Shop windows with rounded bays, angled bays or no bays at all. Upper floor Regency windows mingling with Baroque and the rest, a rare oriel in the Market Place achieving most prominence. Yet despite such diversity, the units blended into a whole at once pleasing and harmonious, as is the way in old English towns.

7

An observant stranger would have been struck by the number of licensed premises. They totalled 26, a prodigious number for a population of three and a half thousand. And they came in infinite variety, from roomy hotels patronised by commercial travellers (not then enjoying the perquisite of a company car) to single public-roomed ale houses. Such abundance deserves listing:

Angel	Garibaldi	Red Lion
Black Swan	Greyhound	Reindeer
Boar's Head	Great Northern	Rodney
Bull	King's Head	Saracen's Head
Cross Keys	Lord Raglan	Ship
Cross Roads	Nag's Head	Vine Bar
Crown	New Inn	Vine Tavern
Fighting Cocks	Plough	White Hart
Fleece	Punch House	

And there was a temperance hotel, the Imperial, that was also favoured by commercial gentlemen.

According to *White's 1856 Lincolnshire*, the town then had 20 inns and taverns and 24 beer-houses. At the 1851 census the population was a little over 5000, making an average of 1 public house per 114 inhabitants. Comparison with the 1920s position (1 for every 130) showed that since the mid-19th century heyday, when the town staged the biggest horse fair in the world, the average had changed comparatively little. White named only the 20 inns and taverns, 16 of which were still in business in the 1920s. The carriage-wide arches of the defunct 4, whose accommodation had been converted to dwelling and/or trade use, betrayed their former status. One of them had its name perpetuated, its stables becoming garages and known as Back Horse Yard. Another, the George Inn, where George Borrow's stay of 1822 was immortalised in the pages of his *Romany Eye*, became the town's post office for decades before a new one was built in the late 'Twenties.

In that decade the still generous quantity of licensed houses did not betoken widespread drunkenness; times were hard and money tight. Only the larger hotels could maintain a whole-time proprietor or manager. As often as not small inns were run by married couples when the man worked at another daytime job and the wife coped single handed with midday trade. Between the wars these local part-time landlords included a cobbler, a carpenter, a railway signalman and an insurance clerk.

During these years too 'free' houses became fewer and fewer and inn signs carrying the names of Grantham, Grimsby and Newark breweries ever more common. Being 'tied' to one brewer did not, however, restrict activities in other respects. The Cross Keys, for instance, remained the branch headquarters of the Ancient Order of Foresters, the Vine Tavern and Black Swan the rallying points of the two football clubs. The Foresters was one of several like organisations so using a public house, and were collectively known as sick and dividing clubs. Members paid a small weekly sum and, if falling ill, received financial help, a boon in pre-Welfare state times when wages often stopped during illness.

Only the Rodney could dispute the Bull's claim to being the town's most notable and commodious hotel and it repaid inspection. A steep, unevenly tiled roof containing three unevenly spaced dormers topped a stuccoed frontage where, at first floor height, a golden rampant bull was embedded in a cavity. Over the archway a magnificent globular gas lamp was suspended, its intricately patterned arm as convoluted as a French horn. At the frontage's southern end the hotel assembly rooms' window — the largest in town — had a little gas lamp under it. The archway led to a partly cobbled yard which ran between lines of outbuildings whose differing heights and projections were the result of gradual development long ago. The yard widened so considerably that a motor repairer happily took up residence there near to the hotel's rear entrance.

The Bull as a whole evoked an atmosphere of coaching days, Regency bucks, illustrations by Phiz, warming pans, churchwarden pipes and mammoth roasts served by buxom wenches. How well it fitted into its surroundings and how well, too, did the little thatched King's Head opposite.

I make it that in the 'Twenties the town possessed around a hundred shops. They were most noticeably a more or less solid formation along the Bull Ring and High Street and into the Market Place with several along streets abutting: East and South Streets into the Bull Ring and Bridge Street into the Market Place. All the same, a proportion were sited away from the town centre, usually general stores serving peripheral localities.

Food shops predominated — there were 10 bakers and confectioners, 9 grocers, 4 greengrocers, 6 butchers and 3 pork butchers. But the largest individual category, clothing and outfitting, numbered 14 taking into account everything from baby linen shops to those catering for adults. Two of these that linger in memory were at either end of the main concentration specialising in mature women's apparel. Each was run by a pair of spinster sisters, each had massive whalebone corsets as staple window exhibits. It is to be supposed both enjoyed a fair trade in thick ("sensible") woollen underwear in season.

The half dozen or so sweet shops naturally held much interest. The one I patronised (because en route to and from school) was archetypal. A thought shabby, one's entrance heralded by the jangling bell attached to an overworked door, labelled glass bottles — butterscotch, rum and butters, bullseyes, toffees, aniseed balls, liquorice allsorts — on the shelves. Readier to hand on the counter, ha'penny and penny items: Barrett's sugary red tipped "Gold Flake Sweet Cigarettes" five to a packet, lengthy jet black strips of spanish half an inch wide, in spanish also another popular form — a hollow tube thrust into a little cylinder through which sherbet was sucked and then tube and cylinder consumed as well. A window crammed with samples of delights to be found within, illumined on dark evenings by a single lowly suspended gas globe; protected in summer with an external tautly stretched canvas bearing the words "Packer's Chocolates". The lady shopkeeper, archetypal too: elderly, white haired, be-spectacled, kindly.

In pre-school days personal acquaintance with the town shops was provided

Halfway up "... the steep hill to the west of the little town" in the mid-1930s.

MAREHAM ON THE HILL DAIRY FARM.   L. WINGATE - PROPRIETOR.
ORDERS LEFT AT 31 EAST STREET, HORNCASTLE, WILL BE PROMPTLY DELIVERED.

NOT LOST, BUT
GONE BEFORE.
on OGDEN'S 'Guinea-Gold'
Cigarettes.

High Street, Horncastle.

Grandad (fourth from left) and workmates in Edwardian days.

by Grandma. On market days, Saturday, we visited the butcher, on other afternoons shops dealing in clothing and kindred requirements. There was a wool shop, for instance, presided over by a lady of notable girth. She sat behind her counter like an immobile queen bee directing an obsequious assistant in the matter of customers' wants. Then Mrs. Daubney, milliner and dressmaker, at the time the local high priestess of haute couture, who had premises extending over two floors. The ground floor, devoted mainly to display, had at its end a staircase with — sophisticated touch — a large potted palm on the landing. The stairs led to the living quarters but the room over the shop was a trying-on salon where customers preened before mirrors to Mrs. Daubney's accompanying commentary. Fortunately the salon had an agreeable distraction: the window afforded a view of all the Market Place's placid activity. Sober suited men and long skirted women going in and out of shops, banks and Post Office, carts rattling over stone setts on which horses' hooves sometimes made diverting sparks, an occasional motor vehicle still rare enough to warrant attention.

But Robinson Bros., general drapers and soft furnishers, received more of our visits than any. A deep, dusky cavern of a shop, dusky even in summer because an awning spanned the pavement outside guarding display windows from the sun's rays. Inside on both sides of the entrance stood upended rolls of carpet and linoleum like so many sentinels, the strong greeting smell an amalgam of carpet, linoleum, cloth and camphor getting more pronounced as one advanced. The shop had three parts — firstly the floor covering section, then a slight bend into a general department and, finally, the millinery. After this point the shop ended and was the domain of young seamstresses usually filling in the years between school leaving and marriage.

Grandma usually made for the middle section where anything from a packet of pins to a three-piece man's suit could be bought. There she would take a seat on a high cane-bottomed chair at a counter that received natural light from a glazed roof overhead (there must have been a single storey projection to account for the roof's existence). The counter's many scars and embedded brass rule's half obliterated markings showed that it had seen much service. Opposite the counter in one corner stood a tall-chimneyed stove, in operation apt to splutter asthmatically and with its warmth accentuate the shop aroma.

Grandma, in her element, did not long engage an assistant in small talk. Soon she was engrossed in matching buttons and threads, comparing cloth colours, feeling the quality and thickness of materials, enquiring prices. In the background hovered the proprietory brothers, Mr. Fred and Mr. Tom. They were a contrasting pair: gingery Mr. Fred, lined face somewhat worried looking; Mr. Tom, plumper and benign, hair and moustache comparable in snowy whiteness to those shown in contemporary Lloyd George photographs. When Grandma had finally decided on the day's purchases one or both would advance, rubbing hands in the then approved manner, to pass the time of day. There was no shortage of topics. The trio were from the same generation, were assured (Grandma held unshakeable views on many subjects, the Robinsons had established shopkeepers' aplomb), all were stout Wesleyans and — one might reasonably guess — of like political persuasion.

13

Long after the initiation into the questionable delights and likely boredoms of shopping were solo visits to a barber. At four or five weekly intervals came the adult edict one's hair must be cut. All four gents' hairdressers were manned by people with a fine conversational line on weather, harvest and farming topics, days gone by, politics (provided the company's leanings were known and did not include men of differing persuasions) and local events (particularly sport). And, I am sure, local scandal (but not in the presence of child customers and any women within earshot). Mr. Cammack, who had been paid the necessary few coppers earlier in case I lost them, could even conjure talk from an adult-shy eight year old. It went something like this.

Mr. Cammack "They say the new Grammar School master is a good centre-half."

Me (faintly) "Yes, Mr. Cammack."

Mr. Cammack "Did you see him play against Cranwell RAF?"

Me (not quite so faintly, flattered to be addressed by a grown-up on so important a matter) "Yes, Mr. Cammack."

Mr. Cammack "What did you think?"

Then, with a small client suitably emboldened, the talk flowed.

Regularly awaiting Mr. Cammack's ministrations every month or so enabled the study of a large framed 1900s advertisement on the wall near the saloon door. It depicted a scene in church. A lady in sweeping skirts and wearing a large hat stood demurely holding an opened hymn book, by her side her Eton jacketed son frantically fumbling in his trouser pocket. In front of him a corpulent moustachioed man wearing pince-nez stood, impatiently thrusting a collection bag towards the embarrassed boy. The caption underneath read "Not lost but gone before on Ogden's Guinea-Gold Cigarettes."

In remembering sounds those of rippling water are second only to horses' hooves. Two rivers wound their separate ways from the Wolds to the town eventually to join there, originally at the tongue of land between them. Usually the rivers were innocuous enough — clear streams where in the warm months you could see tiny fish jerkily darting above smoothed pebbles. Then you often paddled in the shallows, shorts rolled to the crotch, catching tiddlers with a white cotton-mesh net attached to a bamboo stick, a possession equally useful for trapping butterflies. But only in certain shallows: it was a part of local boy lore to know where dangerous waters were.

The rivers' innocence was deceptive. Foretastes of possible trouble occurred in times of heavy rains or thawing snow. Then they swelled into swift moving, swirling torrents, dirt brown in colour, passing ominously close to the top of the arches under both main bridges. Twice in living memory, not long after each world war, deluges in the Wolds caused floods that devastated the town. The first disaster was in 1920 and for decades afterwards when 'the flood' was mentioned everyone knew the speaker was not referring to Noah's flood. Around 1922 journeys to and from school were enlivened by the sight of muscular men standing in the river digging out silt with hefty shovels. These men seemed to embody a height of masculine attainment with their apparent ease in wielding the shovels, glistening thigh-high wading boots and strange oaths. After the second flood forty years later, modern engineering supplied a different solution, the river bed being dredged and concreted, and this combined with other works may have forestalled future disasters.

The 1922 watching of river workers' rites was an adult occupation too, especially when operations were near the Town (south) bridge, in many ways the town's focal point. Here loungers gathered, here much male talk happened — desultory or earnest, argumentative and reminiscent. Rails either side of the bridge parallel to the river and used at Horse Fairs for tethering horses, made ideal back rests or seats, posteriors on the top rail and heels anchored on the lower. Here the familiar one legged ex-serviceman smoked a reflective pipe with or without company, his crutches resting on the rails. Our favourite position was on the bridge itself watching the water swirl beneath, hands dangling between the iron railings. And then leap frogging over the bollards at either end, light 'Twenties traffic permitting such sport.

And what of aromas? Two predominate in recollection: gas and leather.

The small gasometer, sited in the appropriate but prosaically named Gas Street, served a street lighting system fickle to say the least. The lamps were inclined to emit a spluttering wheeze and give a light that dimmed and brightened in turn. This was often true of the lamp nearest to our house (one, it appeared, Grandma successfully campaigned to have installed) whose light would often wax and wane with the frequency of a rotating lighthouse beam. It followed that, in so indifferent a system, much repair work was needed and the sight of gasmen trundling their handcart to the latest emergency common. In fairness, though, it must be recorded gas smells were not continuously in evidence. For one thing the gasmen were diligent, for another lamps were not lit in the summer months.

No such close season applied to leathery smells, either in town or at home. The works gave out a pungency the whole year through as did its waterside offshoot where Grandad worked. And the open doors of two saddlers shops, ringed by halters, traces, bridles and footballs, broadcast a more refined leather odour interlarded with dubbing.

Inevitably Grandad brought the odour home. He was a currier — one who dressed and coloured leather after tanning — and his working clothes and faithful bowler were impregnated with it. No-one, however, suffered any discomfort: through constant exposure the odour had become no more noticeable than the familiar tick of the living room clock.

Grandad's brother, a boot repairer, provided a further leathery link. He occupied a shop famed far beyond the town's boundaries because in Victorian times a previous tenant had combined cobbling with the post of public hangman. The shop itself was unremarkable but had passed into legend along with the hangman himself.

TWO : THE NATIVES ARE FRIENDLY

The Grammar School's most recent historian tells of an old boy remarking how happy he had been and how kind everyone was in his schooldays during the 'Twenties. The historian properly comments that neither happiness nor kindness are primary features of good education and may, indeed, be a disincentive to it. However, the comment may also be properly made that, in a wider context, kindness is to be cherished.

Looking back, I am sure kindness was the community's outstanding characteristic. A newcomer found the entrée into social, sporting, cultural and religious activities extremely easy. Locals deliberately sought his or her participation and, if hailing from outside Lincolnshire, treated differences in speech and custom respectfully and rarely, if ever, derisively. To a newcomer from, say, the South, such treatment must have been astonishing.

A foreigner's sporting abilities were often valued — at any rate initially — as superior to a native's homebred ones, for another community trait was modesty. Pride (more often termed 'swank', a then vogue word) ranked as chief of the seven deadly sins. In a place small enough for everyone to know everybody else, people were lynx-eyed in noting any semblance of affectation. Anyone who achieved some success — a promotion at work, an examination pass — would be especially watched. But inbred modesty ensured few could be justifiably accused of swank as they visibly kept a common touch.

Perhaps less admirably we were great spectators. As a dialect writer put it, "Lincolnshire people always stands up and 'es a good gawp". 'Gawping' went beyond the mere transitory taking-in of a scene, person or object. It constituted a slow, unhurried mental indexing so thorough that instant recall could be indulged years afterwards.

In fine then the general demeanour may be described as self effacing with a readiness to smile, the smile often a little shy or wry. And, noticeably, a compulsive tendency to stand and stare.

Somewhat different slants have appeared. It was said Lincolnshire folk possessed a slightly harsh — almost North Country — speech, sardonic humour, commercial realism and a capacity for making money, and were uncompromising, downright, independent and a little dour. This list has been quoted approvingly with an additional idea that these qualities applied equally to Yorkshiremen in the East Riding. The similarity stemmed, the reasoning went on, from a common Danish ancestry and proved the River Humber united rather than divided Yellowbellies and Tykes.

Whilst it cannot be gainsaid their ideas contained elements of truth, a feeling persists that neither writer hailed from the area and had only a 'passing through' acquaintance with it. Both books appeared long before the shotgun marriage of the East Riding and North Lincolnshire to form a new Humberside administrative county. A perusal of the many letters to the press on the union from both sides of the river might have given the river-uniting theorist pause. The letters, almost wholly hostile to the union, mention speech differences, which are self evident, and traditions, which are not (at least to a superficial experience).

Geographically, too, the writers' reasoning is suspect. Lincolnshire regionally has invariably been placed in the East Midlands. This has been so from early times when it was part of Mercia (Yorkshire being in Northumbria) to the present-day gas and electricity boards. A third writer well illustrated the matter in 1962. He had returned to England after a 12-year exile and wrote a re-appraisement of the ever topical North vs. South divide. In making his division Lincolnshire was specifically mentioned as having more in common with East Anglia than Yorkshire on a "common sense geography" principle. Again, then, a consistently applied verdict: the North starts on the northern bank of the Humber.

Now, as this manuscript is being revised (May 1993), an investigation into the possibility of returning to traditional Lincolnshire and Yorkshire boundaries has been ordered. Newspaper and radio polls have shown that, of the people who voted, an overwhelming number preferred the old boundaries. May their voices be heard!

That thorny, thankless subject, class. Working-class children did not recognise the manifold gradings and shadings of the English class system before, say, entering Grammar or High School. Hitherto the environment was taken for granted; experience taught which people outside home circles were approachable, and family ideas on outsiders' place in the scheme of things were unconsciously imbibed. Later, wonderingly, one found these outsiders did not necessarily occupy the pigeon-holes older folk had suggested.

In retrospect our town does not seem to have been overly class-ridden. The tempo of life in the 1920s did not match that of the late twentieth century. The 'Roaring Twenties' tag, beloved by journalists, hardly applied to a small East Midlands community, and the urge to claw a way up the social ladder exceptional. Two reasons may be advanced: the population's overwhelmingly artisan/labouring character and the previously mentioned aversion to ostentation.

The completely leisured, not counting moderately well circumstanced retired folk, were few. They accepted presidencies of various bodies (e.g. dramatic society and angling club), donated to good causes, sometimes served as magistrates. They led easy lives that the average workaday inhabitant neither understood nor particularly envied. A well-off widow employed the largest domestic staff: two maids living in plus a married couple living nearby, the wife acting as cook/housekeeper, her husband as gardener/groom. His duties included the tending of two caged, often fiercely baying, Alsatians that were surprisingly docile when taken out singly by their mistress on her daily strolls. A leisured gentleman, spiritualist and wireless pioneer (mammoth aerials behind his house were famous landmarks) died during the decade, his name perpetuated by several bequests including annual prizes to chosen school children.

17

The leisured were joined in the top strata by the professions, ministers of religion, neighbouring farmers, bank managers and the owners of the largest businesses. Relative affluence could be roughly gauged, of course, by the size of house and number of domestic staff employed therein. Larger houses were not always the most comfortable. If old they were inclined to have high ceilings and stone-flagged kitchens and must have been dauntingly cold in those pre-central heating winters.

Domestic service was not yet regarded as demeaning. Though servants were not so plentiful as in pre-1914 days, there still appeared to be an adequate pool. Even people of lesser affluence were able to find women wishing to earn a few shillings assisting with the heaviest cleaning and wash day chores. Families which supplied domestics were usually the least well-off. But neither this nor any other fact prevented everyone mingling at garden fête, jumble sale, concert or any other gathering without condescension from employers and servility from employed. In short, an unknowing carrying out of Burns's maxim "A man's a man for a' that".

Broadly, as elsewhere, the political syndrome ran Church of England = Conservative and Wesleyan Methodist = Liberal. The other denominations with smaller congregations were not so readily definable but would be more likely to favour the Liberal cause.

Our constituency was a far flung territory of small towns, variously sized villages and hamlets and one appreciable seaside resort. The Conservatives and Liberals had it all to themselves. Both parties won the seat during the decade and Labour then never achieved a significant poll. The Grammar School provided an illustration of Labour's scant following in the 1929 election. We became political for election day only and sported party rosettes or ribbons —almost certainly in every case revealing the allegiances of our families. (Incidentally, the colours were not those nowadays associated with the respective parties but were pink for Conservative, blue for Liberal and yellow for Labour). Not surprisingly in a school composed largely of farmers' and tradesmens' offspring, Conservative pink swamped the rest. The comparative few of us wearing blue felt somewhat overwhelmed and we tended to herd together at break times like old time christians in a pagan city. But feelings of being outnumbered were as nothing to those of the two boys who bravely wore Labour yellow.

Election times added some mites to the folklore fund. Tales of triumphant or shouted down hecklers at the well attended candidates' meetings, or inveterate Liberals riding to polling booths in Conservative cars and vice versa — there were no Labour cars. And, most notorious, of the employer who told each employee individually how he should vote. This last may or may not have been apocryphal, but it did not go without comment that his workmen wore rosettes of the required hue, calling to mind the line in Tennysons's Northern Farmer: "Thaw a knaws I hallus voated wi' Squoire an' choorch an' staate". (You know I always voted with the Squire and church and state).

At opposite ends of the Market Place stood the Liberal and Conservative clubs, from the upper windows of which successful candidates received acclaim from the faithful after the result had been declared. Ever mindful of the deferential and working class vote, the Conservatives had made their working men's club the best in the district. The billiard tables were immaculate, several coal fires blazed the warmest welcome in cold months. Its reading room held a rich assortment — national dailies (but only those of Tory persuasion), the famous monthly fiction magazines (*Strand*, *Pearson's*, *Windsor*, *World Wide*), smart periodicals such as *The Illustrated London News* and *Tatler* and, nearer to members' concerns, *Exchange and Mart*. Probably most members voted Tory anyway, but the club's attractions may have swayed the less committed to do so.

With the newfangled wireless in its infancy and television thirty years away, people tended to be less conformist in outlook and appearance. True, they had newspapers and the ever popular cinema, but the first had little influence and films depicted lives remote from the reality most knew.

In our town divergences from the norm were common enough, and often long standing enough, to be unremarkable. A tailor's habitual wearing of a swallow-tailed coat — a style long outmoded for day clothes — caused no comment. Nor did another tailor's partiality for riding breeches and his appearance in advertisement photographs so clad (he was not a horseman). Another sartorial quirk — a large jovial townsman, invariably accompanied by a dog proportionately large, assumed a hat much nearer to stetson than trilby dimensions.

Individuals emerged as real characters from all manner of attributes. From a profitable hobby: the postman who earned a deserved fame for intricate gramophone and clock repairs. From idiosyncrasy: the lady who kept a sheep as a house pet. Or from a job: the town crier. He wore no regalia when carrying out his duties; a short, tubby, cloth-capped figure clanging an outside handbell and giving vent to an outside voice that emerged from under a quivering moustache. Every sentence had a cadence and sing-song delivery that did not aid clarity. It therefore behoved bystanders wishing to know precisely what the crier had proclaimed to enquire elsewhere.

Earliest journeys to and from school were enlivened by two other characters. An old farmer of undiminished testy temperament lived en route. He shared his semi-retirement with a dog, an indeterminate number of chickens, geese and pigs and a couple of milch-cows. He had a special aversion to boys who, knowing this, delighted in shouting "Owd Daddy English" through his letter-box. Owd English would burst forth; fat, bald, flannel shirted, hugely pot-bellied, protruding tongue aquiver, corduroys held up by both belt and braces and tied at the knee with binder twine. He would pursue for a few yards before heaving to a cursing, spluttering halt, his unknown tormentor out of sight. A simple pleasure, but satisfying.

Near to Owd English lived someone quite different, a strange being almost a recluse. His first name was Marmaduke, which in itself set him apart, and he had published poetry using the pseudonym Nimrod. An inappropriate one, it must be said, as Nimrod was a mighty hunter and warrior. Truth to tell we were rather frightened of Marmaduke, whose white beard-fringed face topped by a be-tasselled Victorian smoking cap could occasionally be seen at an upstairs window. But our fears were groundless for he was a sick and dying man.

Perhaps best known of all a local lady of pleasure, bawdy, ever laughing and likely good hearted. An apochryphal story about her went the rounds. One night a client knocked at her door. No reply. He knocked again. Still no reply. He knocked a third time more loudly. An upstairs window opened and the lady's tousled head appeared.

"Who's that?" she asked crossly.

He told her.

"Well, yu'll ha' to cum back laater — yer dad's 'ere!"

Tailors who wore swallow-tailed jackets or riding breeches and gentlemen wearing stetsons were exceptional. Partly through limited means and partly through natural conservatism the adult male population's apparel had an unexciting sameness. For Sunday best, dark suits were favoured with navy blue serge as the most popular. This was not a material of unalloyed excellence as it grew shiny at elbow and seat as time passed. Alternatively there was dark brown, a colour much favoured in house paintwork too. Suits were invariably three piece, the waistcoat spanned frontally by a pocket-to-pocket watch chain. By the middle 'Twenties, though, many younger men had taken to the new gaudy Fair Isle pullovers and exchanged pocket watches for wrist watches. Black or brown boots were more common than shoes early in the decade, but shoes had come into their own by the end of it. Similarly the ubiquitous flannel shirt and rounded celluloid collar were, by around 1927, being replaced by patterned cotton shirts and matching collars. And about that time Oxford bags were *de rigueur* for the trend conscious young.

As for hair styles, the favourite was that made popular by Army officers

On the Bain, Horncastle.

during the Great War — combed straight back from the forehead. whatever the style, straight back or parted, the hair usually had a spectacular gloss induced by a lavish application of brilliantine. Moustaches were prevalent among the middle-aged and elderly but rarely grown by young men. However, pencil-thin 'gigolo' moustaches and accompanying sideburns were not unknown, though considered daring. By the 1920s beards had become nearly extinct, a rare survival being the station master's, whose neatly trimmed whiskers and moustache inevitably brought the reigning George V to mind.

Although for headgear trilby and bowler had plenty of adherents, neither could compete numerically with the cloth cap. Not only did it do duty for work but its owner usually had another for 'best'. Particularly important was the manner of wearing. Seldom if ever was it worn 'straight' in the way adopted by county and pseudo-county types when it became fashionable shortly after World War 2 — this would have been considered somewhat odd. Between the wars caps were worn at a slant, to right or left according to preference, with the rear pulled over like a Basque's beret. This way of cap wearing was tacitly accepted as an individual staking of masculinity, a tribal sign of 'one of the boys'. The fashion of going hatless did not transpire until the 'Thirties, coinciding with the sun tan cult. Earlier baring one's skull to the summer sun was thought to be an open invitation to sunstroke.

Women were, of course, clothes conscious and, despite limited purses, contrived to keep in fashion — or rather the younger ones did. They readily adopted the cloche hats and short tube-like dresses of the emancipated 'Twenties flapper. Their mothers and grandmothers tut-tutted and kept to lisle stockings and mid-calf skirts. These elders were not so conservative in hair styles, however, and most had their hair bobbed or shingled even if none emulated the young's Eton crop.

So numerous were nicknames that it seemed a plot existed to boycott perfectly good, often succinct and manageable christian names. But this applied almost wholly to men and boys although a wife might be referred to as Mrs. Punch or Mrs. whatever appellation her husband rejoiced under. The invention or application of nicknames was not the exclusive privilege of any one age group but extended throughout the male population.

The most obvious were those in nation-wide use (Wiffles for Wilfred, Eggy — Eric, Chuck — Charlie, Lal — Leslie, Jacko — Jack). We had others with a plain or tenuous connection to the original (Ally — Harold, Colly —Collinson, Aimy — Alfred, but this might have evolved from his surname). Far from obvious were Robin (for a George), Pat (for a Percy), Ike (for an Ernest), and Mick used for both a George and a Bert.

Surnames sometimes received a new forename that brought a pleasing alliteration: Fungzer, Perry, Mucker and Topper all followed in the wake of a pleasant sounding Jammy Jarvis. A choice few were especially euphonic as the first two letters coincided (Clonk, Grun, Grundy, Crocker and Trunky). Some were a direct play on the surname (Giddy, Rusty, Eppy, Twaller and Tacker).

Trades and callings denoted a number: Mainspring and Clocky for a couple of jeweller-cum-timepiece repairers, the latter also alliterative. A baker was

Buns, a furnisher Chairleg, a greengrocer Tartar, a game dealer Trapper, a road worker Cobbles, the gunsmith Gunner. Taxi for a local car driver was too obvious to be up to standard, as was Butcher (except for the fact he was not of that vocation!). Of implements signified, Shovel and Brush were appropriate, Bucket and Barrel less so.

Living things gave their names to a quota: Chick, Ducks, Sparrow, Chucky, Bunny, Donkey, Puppy, Tadpole, Buck and two unfortunates labelled Monkey. Eatables included Pudding, Custard, Candy, Sausage and Pod. Radish and Suet derived from their owner's surnames. Cabbo may have been short for cabbage. The man's name was Lettice, near enough to lettuce to induce an 'opposite' nickname. (At the Grammar school we similarly had a "Sugar" Buttery).

Personal characteristics inevitably spawned many a name — Darky, Porky, Slogger, Scorcher, Snowy, Tot, Tich and Merry are self-explanatory or nearly so. Not so the two Soapys, Boxer (a large bus driver), Double (one with a speech impediment) Togger (a natty dresser) and Felix, an elderly clergyman of stiff gait whose residence coincided with the popular song "Felix Kept On Walking", in celebration of Felix, the film cartoon cat. Unflattering sobriquets were Loony, whose sole crime was an animated demeanour, Dodger, Weary and Stinker. A probably hurtful one, Doggy, stemmed from the youth's naturally doleful countenance. Punch was a little bald man with a hook nose and his nickname was singularly apt. Apt too (if a derivative of pompous) was Pompey, a stout man of magisterial bearing. A local preacher had two cognomens — Pilgrim for his fundamentalist outpourings and Cup o' Tea for a large tea intake when travelling in the surrounding villages. Plum and Tancy came from owning the same surnames as, respectively, a famous cricketer and boxer of the day, and Tishy from a contemporary racehorse.

Some, although proper words, defy rational explanation: Dot, Pinky, Judy, Lila, Sacking, Screw, Neptune, Boss, Bumbler, Chips, Putty (there are two), Teak, Doodles, Rocky and Jigger. Even more irrational is the largest category — nicknames seemingly nonsensical and, to strangers, apparent gibberish: Brum, Wuffy, Chipper, Dusher (father and son), Skimps, Blong, Ingy, Groomy, Rokty, Snig, Bonner, Bimmy, Bish, Tinger, Lally (for an Albert), Ruffy, Pusser, Bomby, Bubs, Champer, Bingy, Dawdy, Tranner (father and son), Brib, two unrelated Noggers, Rompty, Gawker (father and son), Pro, Tut, Jonty, Giggums, Razzo, Wo, Stutch, Midder, Shep, Manny, Froz, Checky, Shanner, Riah, Jiffler, Babs, Scrim, Quebby, Dutchy, Nutty, Etty (there were three), Peeny, Nunk, Nimby, Prinny, Crutey, Grabber, Bunt and two unrelated Chings.

There remains the few appellations applied to females. Only five can be recalled. There were for schoolgirls: Pussy, Spodge and Tilly (a variation of Hilda). The others, Sally and Polly, related to Grammer School mistresses.

For the vast majority of families money was far from plentiful and a general agreement prevailed that, come what may, two concerns must come first —fuel and food. So a full coalhouse and an adequately stocked larder showed a family's proper sense of priorities, while another's seeming large expenditure on "gaddin' about" earned disapproval from the censorious. Fortunately coal and food were cheap and prudent folk usually contrived an occasional outing though not with the regularity of the feckless.

With food's cheapness went a widespread ability to cook well. From time immemorial mothers had passed on recipes and demonstrated culinary skills to their daughters. Being realists, mothers anticipated their daughters would marry into the same income group as themselves, therefore having need of these skills. Marriage for a girl then still entailed leaving her job and devoting herself entirely to housewifely duties. For her, with convenience foods still to be invented, domestic refrigeration not yet available, there hovered the powerful, if invisible, fact of tradition.

So cooking skills there had to be. Besides money shortage the means of cooking in many houses had not changed for generations. Although the town had gas, gas cookers were not in universal use, and the electricity supply did not reach us until 1933. Many women used one or a combination of two methods: the the open fire and its side-partner oven and/or a paraffin stove. This last, often a Primus and heavy though quite small, stood a mere nine inches or so with an oval cooking 'platform' at the top roughly three inches across. It seemed reasonably reliable though hardly an aesthetic object and apt to quickly become sooty black. Matches had always to be kept handy, wick constantly trimmed and paraffin level regularly checked but — telling consideration — it was economical to run.

Cooking by means of an open fire meant the household sweltered in warm weather. It also exacted a high degree of ability from the cook. In an archetypal iron range layout the fire would be flanked on one side by the oven and, on the other, by the 'boiler' (a fairly capacious enclosed space containing water heated by the adjacent fire). Coals were raked under the oven and much skill lay in judging temperatures. No woman in my experience relied on any timing device, an occasional glance at a clock sufficing, yet the judgement was unerring no matter whether the oven contained meat, pastry or pudding. Indeed the oven's two shelves often held meat and pudding for the mid-day meal which required differing cooking times. Eulogies have been written on lesser things than Grandma's pastry making abilities. Feather light and delicious, her creations melted in the mouth as delightfully as any choice sweetmeat. Cheese cakes, jam and bakewell tarts, ordinary and plate size, mince pies in season and the rest emerged from her oven unfailingly perfect. And those unforgettable pie crusts that made the fruit or meat underneath seem relatively unimportant! (How fortunate my Mother inherited the gift — and the recipe? — so one's taste buds continued to be pleasured after Grandma died). Grandma's large cakes, also baked weekly, equalled her pastry. In retrospect it can be seen why they were so filling: substantial cakes helped the pastry to last a regulation seven days.

Our brick-floored pantry had to be spacious to contain, besides food, food's incidental utensils and receptacles. The freestanding earthenware bread 'pipkin' could hold four large loaves. Another of similar size but glazed externally stood nearby and was used for preserving eggs in water glass, a process now possibly almost forgotten. The pancheon, a massive earthernware bowl Grandma used when making Christmas puddings or in occasional bread making, occupied one corner. The shelves contained, among other items, the results of half a century's random crockery buying and acquiring through birthday, wedding and holiday presents. There must have been every conceivable size of plate, saucer, dish, cup, mug and beaker; every type of jug from the giant three-pint vessel (thoughtfully filled daily in hot weather with a home made lemon drink) to the small mite used for mint sauce. Glassware occupied one shelf — pint and half-pint tumblers, wine glasses, jugs and carafes in serried ranks. Miscellaneous objects abounded. An exquisite little cut-glass preserves dish, a cruet of boarding house size, a cake dish featuring red roses and the inscription "A Present from Skegness", oddments from the Coronations of Edward VII and George V and many another.

A notable utensil resident in the back kitchen was a cauldron annually pressed into service for jam making. Every jam, marmalade, curd or other suitable jar would be hoarded throughout the year and carefully washed, and on the selected day placed on the kitchen table to await the newly made jam. Grandma, with her customary consummate judgement, cajoled the fire to right heat and staying power, then operations began. It was an arduous stint. The bubbling heaving admixture in the cauldron eventually produced from prepared fruit and sugar had to be continually stirred with a wooden spoon. Grandma sat on the edge of her rocking-chair, forehead moist with sweat, blouse sleeves unbuttoned and rolled to the bend of her thin arms, stirring throughout a long afternoon. On one never forgotten occasion boiling jam, when poured, found a fault in a jar, which split neatly into two pieces, On the principle of waste not, want not, Grandma allowed me to attack the luscious spilled jam with a dessert spoon. On such moments are the best memories built.

If Lincolnshire people had ever decided to deify an animal, that animal would surely have been the pig. The number of styes behind old houses in town and village showed pig keeping had a long tradition, just as the many pork butchers' shops showed a native demand for pork products.

In the villages a pig often constituted part of a farm worker's wages. Therefore its growth — promoted by a household scraps and pig-mash diet —was watched, if not anxiously, certainly with a vested interest fixation. In winter came the killing, a bloody affair performed by an experienced man. He slit the wretched animal's throat and loud, dissenting, piteous squeals rent the normally tranquil air before death brought release.

After the killing hair was removed by means of hot water and purpose-made scraper, the carcass disembowelled and hung from a stout hook to dry out for the better part of twenty-four hours. Then the cutting-up began. Nothing was wasted: liver and lungs were minced and went into pies, ears and feet became brawn, some meat was set aside for sausages and pork-pies. Hams and sides were salted for preserving — the nucleus of the family's meat supply for many months ahead.

Some time later came the making of Lincolnshire's most celebrated dish, stuffed chine. After the salt had been soaked away the chine (i.e. meat from a pig's back) was sliced at quarter-inch intervals and into the resulting grooves went finely chopped parsley. The chine was then placed on a piece of linen which was sewn up and then boiled — often in a copper, a brick-enclosed boiler used on wash days.

My mouth waters as I type!

"You can't beat old fashioned remedies," everybody said. And in those pre-National Health Service days, where a doctor and his consequent bill was often a last resort, so steadfastly held a belief carried a comforting ring.

Old fashioned remedies were called upon to combat any and every minor ailment. Catching a cold portended a pre-bed dose of sweet nitre and tincture of rhubarb, a potion one snuffler at least found singularly displeasing. A cold's legacy, a cough, focused attention on one's chest, which received a mighty rubbing with camphorated oil. Some folk swore that goose grease similarly applied had equal or even more efficacy, Sore throats could be cured according to many old sages by sleeping with a used sock tied round the throat, and they continued to advocate the treatment despite much earthy ribaldry. Their other suggestion (gargling with salt and water) was much more acceptable, however, and was widely thought to be effective.

At the time, because people had an inordinate fear of constipation, children were wont to be dosed with a laxative weekly whether or no their systems really needed it. The rite usually took place on Friday nights as the school week had ended, thus allowing the victim two days to regain normality. Perhaps castor oil was the most favoured but none of the familiar patent laxatives — pills, fruit salts, syrups and the rest — were despised and often used as considered gentler in action. (In the event, a not unchallengeable belief, however).

Patent medicines figured prominently in many a medicine chest. Branded cough mixtures, pick-me-up tablets, cod liver oils, emulsions, ointments, salves and tonics therein nudged plain-labelled chemists' concoctions. The impression is that patent medicines had more adherents in our parents' generation. Their elders (Grandad was a prime example) swore by old remedies such as Friar's Balsam. An exception may have been Clarke's Blood Mixture, if only because of local connection. The story goes that Clarke, a Lincoln pharmacist, marketed the blood mixture using a recipe culled from a doctor's prescription that had been repeatedly sent to his pharmacy.

As to the town's teeth, it sufficed that a couple of dentists from larger places held surgeries two or three times a week. Running up a dental bill came lower in the priorities than for a doctor, and old people especially presented to the world a smile of gaps and worn stumps rather than well preserved teeth. Grandma's panacea for an aching cavity or hollow tooth was to apply sweet nitre to the affected area with the aid of a paper spill. Like many of the folk lore remedies it often worked.

Many old people, particularly the men, seemed to have an ingrained reluctance to seek professional advice and treatment in health matters. The reasons were not always financial but, at least partly untutored persons' reaction to the unknown and fear of official form filling. Grandad, a remarkably healthy example, never visited a dentist or optician in his life. His own molars saw him through a near 84 year span and he took to wearing Grandma's spare pair of spectacles for reading only after reaching his mid-sixties.

Of customs and beliefs there were many. The selection below is representative and it is highly probable that most, or others like them, existed farther afield than the boundaries of Lincolnshire.

Women wore black for at least a year after a bereavement — black hat, costume (or skirt and topcoat), stockings and shoes; the sole permissible relief a white blouse. Bereaved males wore on the jacket sleeve just above the bend of the arm a diamond shaped piece of black cloth or a black band circling the arm.

If given a pen- or clasp-knife the recipient had to give a ha'penny in return otherwise bad luck would ensure.

If a person called at a house during a meal time, he or she would be invited to partake (a custom I recall seeing in an American silent film, so apparently international).

A somewhat excessive fear of sunstroke was one of several health beliefs. Others included an opinion that an ointment or remedial salve should never be applied with an index finger, and a sprained wrist or finger could mean 'guiders' had been put out. (Guiders apparently being essential though rather delicate minor sinews located in the hand only).

Two weather lore beliefs:

Cutlery attracts lightning.

If it starts to rain before 7 a.m. it will clear before 11.00. (Perhaps a 'whistling in the dark to keep up one's spirits' ploy on a wet start to a day out).

It was deemed lucky to be excreted upon a bird, but (in addition to the nation-wide dictum about walking under ladders) unlucky:

1. For a bride and groom to see one another on their wedding day prior to the ceremony.
2. To first see a new moon through glass.
3. To put on and lace the right shoe before the left.
4. To break a mirror of any size (a dread one this, as the term of bad luck lasted seven years).
5. And direst of all — sitting down to a meal with thirteen at the table. (One of the thirteen would die before a year was out).

THREE : LINCOLNSHEER ENGLISH AS IT WAS (AND IS) SPOK'

It has been well said that there is no one solitary Lincolnshire dialect. How could there be in a county of 2662 square miles, the second largest in all England? That encompassed three administrative counties, the smallest of which was larger than Huntingdonshire? That even in the mutilated form imposed by the 1974 boundary changes still covered 2272 square miles in a new administrative county of Lincolnshire?

There are the inevitable shadings into the accents of bordering counties. Notably into the Midlands whine or, deep in Fen country, into high pitched word-telescoping East Anglian. But not, to my thinking, in the north into hard uncompromising Yorkshire, thanks to the wide Humber. However, Mabel Peacock in her book *Tales and Rhymes in the Lindsey Folk-Speech*, which was published in 1886 and sub-titled *North Lincolnshire dialect*, instances the word 'about' as being pronouced 'aboot'. I heard this pronunciation consistently used in East Riding dialect in the late 1930s. And, as will be seen, there are other likenesses.

In our locality the dialect may best be described as mid-Lincolnshire. It owed nothing to Norfolk but had affinities with Notts. But affinities of accent and intonation only. For all Lincolnshire dialects had and have their own unique and rich peculiarities in coined words, vowel usages, syntax and the rest.

In the wider context of nation-wide pronunciation, a magazine in January 1975 deftly identified a basic division. On a map of England was shown how the two pronunciations of the word 'last' were distributed geographically. The divisions could hardly be more tidy. Below a line stretching from Chester to The Wash we get 'larst', above it 'last' with a short A as in apple. Lincolnshire is accordingly the southern-most eastern county in the 'last' division, with only a small segment adjoining Cambridgeshire and Norfolk in the 'larst' camp. It follows that these two ways of pronouncing A in words such as dance, branch, brass and scores more is as recognisable a first clue as any when roughly placing a regional accent.

A case can be made also for another England halving in the northerly use of owt and nowt and the rest's retention of anything and nothing. Lincolnshire coming in the owt/nowt group. There is a slight qualification here regarding mid-Lincs usage: owt sounds like oat and nowt like note rather than the rhyming with out and snout in Yorkshire. A neat way of dividing England into idiomatic thirds occurs in the common-familiarity term employed by matey waitresses and others. In the South it is dear or dearie, in the North luv' and in the Midlands (including Lincs) duck.

To particularise as respects mid-Lincolnshire pronunciation, the following examples show how standard pronunciations are altered, sometimes radically, sometimes slightly.

Animal	Animile
Arms	Airms — a not unique case of the 'ah' sound being replaced. Another instance is 'airf' for half.
Baby	Babby.
Chapel	Chapil.
Chimney	Chimley or Chimbley, which is not peculiar to Lincs. and found in Yorkshire too. In the Hull area there exists a rather similar mispronunciation: the suburb of Anlaby is called Andelby by elderly natives.
Dent	Dint. Which may pose the query, what does the mid-Lincs dialect speaker use for dint in the sense of "by dint of"? The brief answer is the phrase is not used (or I never recall hearing it).
Engine	Ingin'. Our native likes the 'inje' sound. Another example is oringe for orange.
Fork	Ferk. A prime example of the broadest dialect. Similarly, kerk for cork.
Gave	Gev'. Can be said to have two dialect versions as g'ie (give) is often used for gave, albeit ungrammatically.
Grass	Gress.
Jamb	Jaum. An odd rendering of a simple word that is found in the East Riding also.
Open	Oppen.
Quarter	Quahter (to rhyme with barter).
Row (meaning a line)	Raw. An example of a very common facet — craw for crow, blaw for blow and many more.
Scared	Scarred.
Smoke	Smook or smoo'ak.
Swarm	Swahm (to rhyme with arm). Incidentally, the word in my young days was much in vogue in its meaning of ascending: one always "swahmed up a tree" rather than climbed it.
Water	Watter.
Yes	Yiss. Another common feature — the substitution of E by I. So we find git for get, yit for yet, togither, ivver for ever etc. On the other hand E replaces A in much used words such as 'ev (have), 'ed (had) and 'es (has).

French words adopted by the English language but not anglicised in pronunciation did not attract undue maltreatment in the 1920s. Perhaps with 1914/18 Army service so green a memory it is hardly surprising 'depot' and 'corps' should be correctly pronounced. So, too, was 'fête' with just an occasional 'feet' to show local attempts an anglicism still existed. However, here are three consistent deviations:

Charabanc	Sharrabang, which tallied with nation wide usage and which became an accepted anglicised version. In any event a colloquial shortening, 'sharra', was in general use.
Clique	Click. A word in common use together with its off-shoots, clicky and clickish, for folk of elitist tendency.
Reservoir	Resivoy.

In the idom ...

Your Lincolnshire dialect speaker has an inclination to not sound the letter L in mid-word, thus soldier becomes so'jer and shoulder sho'der. Commonly heard because of frequency in converse is 'self' in all its forms: self = sen, himself = 'issen and so on. And, still more common, owd for old, not only ubiquitous in literal meaning but in extra adjectival use in an affectionate way (e.g. "me owd dad"). Owd is also much used as an 'opposite' — "an owd boy", for instance, as often refers to a male child as an elderly gentleman.

Our dialect speaker does not give full value to the end syllable -ward. To him forward is forrad, backwards bakkuds, awkward awkud and towards slurred into tords. But he does like an uncalled-for -ed ending (growed for grew, seed for saw, telled for told), though not in the case of sprinkled where sprunk is the stand-in. His pronouncing of backwards as bakkuds also illustrates another feature — the omission of letter R in mid-word besides maltreating the word in other respects. Thus turnip becomes tonnup, third thodd and murdered mo'der'd.

He likes the sound of letter A (as sounded in 'ash') as a prefix, translating before to a'fore and abide (in the sense of endure) to a'bear. And this prefix even supplants 'on' and 'of' in a'poppos (on purpose) and a'course (of course). Of, indeed, is a word seldom given more than a cursory a' or o' or replaced by 'on', e.g. on 'em for of them, full on for full off. Yet he is partial to off, which frequently replaces going (e.g. off 'ooam for going home). He is more partial still to the word muck. This (or the dialect equivalent, squod) is nearly always preferred to dirt or mud and, in addition, is the synonym for manure. (Muck spreadin', a phrase much loved by rustic-baiting comedians, is actually the serious agricultural operation of impregnating soil with manure). And the word is closely associated with sweat: muck lather — in a sweat, muck sweat —cold sweat. Favoured too is the word clout (pronounced claht), liberally used in all its meanings of a blow, a dish-cloth or rag and a garment — one of the great parrot maxims is still "Ne'er cast a clout till May is out".

Much used is the word over. Besides the customary meanings it often replaces too (e.g. ovver sharpish for too quickly). And the word is specially interesting in having two dialect pronunciations, ovver and ower.

Our friend's talk might give outsiders pause with a number of other words: sneck for latch, backend — autumn, anyrooad — anyway, write — wrote, tittle — tickle, middlin' — fairly, susstificate — certificate and flit for house removal. But the stranger would not be so mystified as with compact little phrases such as:

Fair agged out	Positively tired out.
Agg on	To persuade, encourage. Very like 'egg on' but I am not at all sure our 'agg on' has a kinship.
Gi'en him gyp or belltinker or 'umpty.	Giving him a bad time.
A topcoo'at cowder	A topcoat colder.
A saucy plee-at	Unconsumed food left on a plate when it is thought the person — usually a child — should have eaten.
That 'ow	That way.

Lastly, foreigners might care to note that in Lincolnshire tea is mashed rather than brewed.

Lincolnshire dialect is rich in substitute or invented words. Many have a succinctness rivalling that of the well known Anglo-Saxon four-letter obscenities (without, of course, indelicate meanings). Some examples.

AWMIN'	Lolling lazily.
BATTLETWIG	An earwig.
BESSOCKS	An old woman.
CAT-HAW	The fruit of the hawthorn.
CHELP	Answering back rudely, impertinence.
CHITTER	Mindless chatter.
CLARTY	Sticky, dirty.
CLAT	Rubbish (see also kelter).
COGGLES	Kidney shaped stones used for paving (word obviously derived from cobbles).
CRAWK	Core of an apple.
DACKER	To lessen speed, to abate.
DICKS	Lice. Hence dick-catcher for a school doctor or nurse inspecting children's scalps.
DONNER	A conkers contest word denoting victories; e.g. a Donner 6 meant a chestnut which had successfully destroyed 6 opposing chestnuts.
GANZY	A cardigan or other woollen overgarment (possibly a corruption of Guernsey).
GAWSTER	To laugh loudly and uproariously.
GLEG	To look or stare, usually in inquisitive manner.
HARR	A sea mist. It would appear each county has its own dialect word for sea mist. In Yorkshire, for instance, it is called a rourk.
JIFFLE	To fidget, particularly when sitting.
JOSKIN	A bumpkin. In Lincs. the phrase 'a country joskin' replaced the widely used 'a country bumpkin'. (The wartime RAF equivalent was an even more expressive 'swede basher').

KELCHIN'	Descriptive of heavy rain: "Kelchin' wi' ray'en" translates into "pouring with rain". The natives use tee'aming (teeming) and silin' in this context also.
KELTER	Rubbish.
LUBBARD	Oaf or blockhead, possibly derived from lubber.
MAGG	To gossip. Sometimes interchanged with chitter, but magging is not necessarily aimless.
MARDY	Bad tempered, peevish. Mostly applied to irritable children.
MAWKIN	A silly fellow (Grandma was wont to apply the word to me when an infant and I confused it with parkin —a cake made with treacle). The word is found elsewhere but with the meanings of slovenly woman and scarecrow.
MAWKS	Maggots. The word is used in Yorkshire dialect and has the same meaning.
MAZZLE	Confuse, particularly in the sense of not being able to comprehend or take in a written text or spoken word.
OWRY	Horrible, repulsive.
PAG	A pick-a-back.
SCRAWK	Scratch. Interestingly the Dutch word for graze is schrammen from which an English dialect word for scratch — scrawm — is thought to derive. Scrawk is presumably the Lincs. version of scrawm.
SILE	Pour (with rain). See kelchin' above.
SLIVE	To creep unnoticed. Generally used in a disparaging way and indicative of deceit.
SNICKERSNEEZE	A jocular and half-serious warning, usually to a child, as in "If you do that I'll snickersneeze you", meaning anything from a pretended spanking to a tickle.
SQUOD	Mud, dirt.
STARNEL	A starling.
STEDDLES	Feet. A lesser used Lincs. word for feet was ockerdols. (An old glossary of Lincolnshire dialect gives steddles as meaning 'the foundation of a stack of grain' a meaning I have never personally encountered.)
STITHERUM	A screed, Equally applicable to unduly long speeches and unduly long amounts of the written or printed word.
TAFFLE	Tangle.
TWIZZLIN'	Rotating. Revolving round an axis.
UNEPPEN	Clumsy, ungainly, awkward.
'UTCH UP	To push forward both as regards things and people. Regarding people, a bus conductor's "Pass down, please" to standers in the gangway is a general way of saying 'utch up.
WOWEY	Insipid, dull, lacking interest.

33

WEZZLIN'	Pre-Christmas carol singing by children going from house to house hoping to be rewarded by a few coppers. The word is obviously a form of wassailing.
WONSER	A blow with the hand, either clenched or open.
YUK	Jerk, pull, snatch.

Often slang words familiar over a wider field are used. Among them are: Fizzog (face), Gawp (stare), Grid or Grid-iron (bicycle), Lug-'oles (ears), Obstropolous (a form of obstreperous: unruly, hard to control), Snitch (nose), Tew (to exert fully as in a frequent earthy phrase "... tewin' 'is guts out"), Yawp (a derisive description of someone's singing).

Besides invented words, usually meaningless to people hailing from outside the county, there are 'proper' words given different — sometimes quite different — meanings in Lincolnshire speech. For instance:

BADLY	Poorly in health ("I 'ee-ad owd Tom's badly agg'an").
BAND	String or cord or twine.
DAIRY	Larder or pantry. Usage comes from the days when country dwellings had a large stone-floored pantry, often with north facing windows, devoted to butter- and cheese-making besides storing eatables. Incidentally the builders deserved praise for the remarkable coolness dairies retained even in the hottest weather.
GAIN	Near, close. Its Lincs. usage is well demonstrated in many an overheard conversation. e.g. "'E was gittin' ower gay-en" (He was getting too close).
GOSH	Swim, bathe. I have never been sure whether the word in this context was limited to our district as it does not appear in any glossary I have seen. As might be expected, the local swimming baths had the affectionate title of the Gosh House.
HUNCH	Cold, particularly as regards water and weather. (In actual converse, 'unch, of course).
JEER	Rump, posterior. Usage perhaps obsolete or, at any rate, getting rarer. In my boyhood it seemed to be confined largely to Grandad's generation who could make a sentence such as "I gev' 'im a kick up th'jeer" as strong sounding as if the well known Old English noun had been used.
LEAD (rhyming with need)	Remove, convey, take away (usually by cart). The word in this context mostly used by farm workers, e.g. "We're mucklee-adin' todaaer" (we are carting manure today).
PAD	A footpath.
ROARING	Crying, snivelling. An alternative to roarin' was beallin' which took the place of squealing also.

SINGLING	Hoeing. A farming word that appeared to receive a fillip in the later 1920s with the coming of widespread sugar beet cultivation. "Singlin' bee-at" then became as common a phrase as muck spreadin'.
SWATH	Bacon rind. (Pronounced swoth).
TRAY	Wooden hurdle used for temporary fencing.

The double vowel ...

An outstanding characteristic of Lincolnshire dialect. It can occur in any type of word — noun, verb, adjective or what you will — and even elongate two-letter words. All that is needful is for the word to contain a long vowel sound to which is added a second vowel before or after the legitimate one. Or the double vowel can completely oust the original (e.g. mate below). A selection:

Again	Agee-an
Blazed	Blay-ezed
Boat	Boo-at
Chain	Chee-an
Cheap	Chee-ap
Clothes	Cloo-az (which is very close to the dialect word for field or enclosure: cloo-ass).
Coal	Coo-al
Drove	Droo-av'
Feast	Fee-ast
Forty	Fowerty
Goat	Goo-at
Head	'ee-ad
Heap	'ee-ap
Joke	Joo-ak
Loaf	Loo-af
Local	Loo-acal
Master	Mayester (but just as frequently, mester).
Matc	Mee-at
No	No-ah
Pony	Poo-any
Post	Poo-ast
Race	Ree-ass
So	Soo-ah
Steam	Stee-am
Strange	Stree-ange
Throat	Throo-at
Through	Throo-ah

There are cases where a double vowel treatment occurs in contractions:

Mustn't (must not)	Moo-ant
Won't (will not)	Wee-ant

Word shortenings ...

Few are so far reaching as the well known reduction of 3-syllable potatoes to a 1-syllable 'tates (or, in a Lincs. rendering, a 2-syllable tee-ates). Or in reducing frightened to a very concise frit (a usage in Parliament by our first woman Prime Minister, Margaret Thatcher, a Lincolnshire native, that won wide publicity).

Generally word shortenings take two forms. By the change of a vowel sound often accompanied by the omission of a mid-word consonant. And the telescoping of two-word phrases, sometimes shortened again from an accepted countrywide shortening.

Examples of the first:

Bird	Bodd
Break	Brek
Broke	Brok
Burn	Bon
Dare	Dost (dialect for 'dare not' is dossent)
First	Fost
Furnace	Fonnis
Furniture	Fonnicher
Gave	Gev'
Give	Gi' (to rhyme with the last syllable of tasty)
Make	Mek
Nurse	Noss (in keeping with a very widespread — ? nationwide — abbreviation of horse to hoss)
Shake	Shek
Stone	Stonn
Thirsty	Thosty (similarly Thursday is rendered as Thosdy)
Waken	Wacken (to rhyme with bracken)
Without	Wi'out
Worse	Woss
Worth	Woth (to rhyme with moth)

And three samples of contractions further contracted:

aint	'ent
isn't	'int
wasn't	wa'n't (indistinguishable from want)

In the matter of word endings Lincolnshire dialect is far from being alone in changing -ow to -er, as in these half dozen specimens:

Barrow	Barrer
Meadow	Medder
Sorrow	Sorrer
Willow	Willer
Window	Winder (rhyming with hinder)
Yellow	Yeller

Actually the ow sound does not find much favour elsewhere — glaw for glow and snaw for snow etc.

An -ed ending is sometimes changed to -t as in:

Asked	Ast
Blamed	Blay-emt
Earned	Arnt
Learned	Larnt

Conversely we can get a legitimate -t ending supplanted by —ed. e.g. Catched for caught.

But these and similar ones are perhaps as much incorrect grammar as dialect oddities, in much the same way as an East Riding dialect speaker uses 'tret' for treated.

A word does not necessarily have to possess an -ed ending to receive a -t substitution:

Always	Allust
Behind	Behint
Sold	Sellt (also selled, following the 'rule' of catched for caught above)

And here are three ending oddments:

Claw	Clawk (they love a -k ending!)
Extra	Extry (occasionally Hextry)
Underneath	Undernee-an

"Nar then, Jarge. 'A ya' got that cloo'ass cut yit?" Which, translated to unversally understandable English, would read: "Now then, George. Have you got that field cut yet?"

I heard the question thus phonetically put many years ago to a farm worker neighbour by another farm worker, and it has remained in memory ever since as a prime example of mid-Lincolnshire speech. A changed vowel, a double vowel and a substitute word are all there. Also the local cadence — a fall of pitch in the opening little sentence, rising again in the longer interrogative one that follows.

We never realise until too late what could have been gleaned from older people and was not. How they might have shed light on events long past, on old customs, on speech and its idiomatic derivations. Instead, as always with the young, we are forever looking ahead, absorbed in our own little concerns, indifferent to anything that took place before our own time. Acting, indeed, as if the here and now is all.

So it was between Grandad and myself. However, it is unlikely much was missed in the dialect field. His talk naturally sank into my consciousness from earliest understanding with no knowledge that any part of it was dialect until school teachers applied a corrective.

Born in the town in 1856, there to spend almost all his long life, Grandad spoke the local brand of Lincolnshire patois unadulterated by any outside influence. Its pronunciation, syntax, word usage and cadence came as naturally to him as rolling up his shirt sleeves. So, to the end, to him a photograph was always a likeness, a bowler a 'ard at', a frequent query "Weers me wetch?"

(where's my watch) and a nightly statement before retiring "Ah'm goin' up th'wooden 'ill". And, true mark of the elderly native, to him the nearby village of Scrivelsby was Screelsby and not the received phonetic pronunciation.

FOUR : NO PLACE LIKE HOME

Mother was widowed after little more than two years of marriage and came home to her parents with the pick of her furniture and me a year old. Grandma must have had a ruthless weeding out to accommodate the furniture. It comprised two bedroom suites, two double-beds, an armchair and a sizeable chesterfield. The stairs were found to be too narrow for the passage of the largest wardrobe and it was eventually admitted through a front bedroom window, the frame of which had to be removed. In course of time this exploit entered family legend to rank with a Midlands-based aunt's constantly repeated promise to buy presents for all relatives next time she visited Rugby. Like Billy Bunter's postal-order, the presents never materialised.

In due course this wardrobe turned out to be a highly interesting object. The bottom part was a drawer deep enough to store half a dozen blankets. The door, fronted for its whole length by a mirror, gave access to a dusky interior and a strong smell of camphor. Besides numerous garments — an increasing quantity as none ever seemed to be dispensed with — the wardrobe contained a furled Union Jack propped in a corner and, at one side, a pile of my annuals. These were *Playbox* and *Tiger Tim's* to be later joined by several *Greyfriars' Holiday Annuals*. The Union Jack had been bought for me to wave at the town's victory parade in 1919. It did not get a second public airing until 1935, when it protruded through an upstairs window, limply wafted by gentle May air, in celebration of the King George V Silver Jubilee.

Our house formed the centre of a terrace of three and was deceptively the largest. The end ones were set forward to ours and were fascia-boarded front and rear in upturned-V fashion. Our house linked them like the base of a rather squat letter U. The houses were old, brickwork and pantiles much weathered by a century of East coast and prevailing winds. They stood well back from the road on land distinctly lower which had many generations before been the site of a gravel pit. Although there had never been any gravel extracted during the lifetime of anybody living in the 1920s, locals still referred to the houses collectively as "the Gravelpits". Much to Grandma's disgust, incidentally. Through a bequest she owned all three and was at great pains to point out the official title inscribed on a little board attached to the gate: "Rose Cottages". But her remonstrances made no difference; "the Gravelpits" it had always been and would continue to be. And so, for Grandma, this misnaming remained a constant grievance like Grandad's extended Saturday after-work visit to the Cross Keys and me laying stomach-down on the Kitchen hearthrug reading, impeding access to the oven.

Our parlour was always called "The Room", the capital letters inferred in conversation as surely as when talking about the Armistice or the Chapel. This followed from a tacit assumption of its self-evident importance as opposed to, say, the coalhouse, which deserved only a small first letter. Certainly the Room had its points. Like countless other modest parlours it contained the choicest family possessions lovingly hoarded over the years. Here, too, the post-meal venue for annual festivities. Snug Christmases when relatives swelled our ranks; where digestions were revived, nuts cracked, crackers pulled, sweets sucked, cards played and children permitted to stay up abnormally late. Easters with weather still chilly enough to well justify a cheerful fire although lengthening daylight hours promised oncoming warmer months. Whitsun and August bank holidays when we might repair to the Room after 'Walking round the Globe' (up to High Toynton, a short way along Greetham Lane, then down a long bridle path to emerge in the town at Green Lane — at the time itself tantamount to a bridle path — and back home). And the Room, too, likely a spot as anywhere for Grandad to make the same remark to visiting relatives at least once — "There'll be a lot o' folk up an' down the country this 'oliday time". Did he, I now wonder, use this as a conversation opener when he and a favourite son-in-law adjourned to the Cross Keys for a pre-dinner beer?

The twelve-foot square Room's wonder lay in the amount of furniture it contained, apparently without strain. Door and fireplace accounted for one wall and round the others were ranged an upright piano, a bamboo table that supported our gramophone, a bureau, a chiffonier and the famous chesterfield capable of seating four adults comfortably. Sundry chairs and a moderately sized round table occupied the centre. Two other items deserve mention: a shiny ebony box normally found under the chesterfield and a family album. The box held a miscellany of family documents — birth certificates, insurance policies, Grandad's Indenture of Apprenticeship dated 1872 and so on, all looking terribly official. The family album resided on the table and had probably done so from time immemorial. None of the photographs between its thick tooled covers dated from later than the 'Nineties and most harked back to photography's early days. Their subjects stood stiff and unrelaxed. The earliest showed women in voluminous skirts, little lace caps on ringleted heads; frockcoated men with copious whiskers. The later ones featured groups and individuals just as consciously posed, men's cravats now replaced by high celluloid collars and narrow ties; women with hats a foot and a half wide and leg-of-mutton sleeves.

The chiffonier was the apple of Grandma's eye. (And was always called the chiffonier, correctly pronounced, and never sideboard). It stood proud, polished and cosseted, cherished as a favourite child. On the ledge above its bevel-edged mirror were her choicest small ornaments. Behind its ornately carved doors were shelves filled with equipment for special occasions — best linen and lace tablecloths, the best canteen of cutlery, a 'silver' teapot and stand and cake dish, a beautiful bone china tea service.

The gramophone also ranked high in Grandma's affections. She would sit entranced for hours while we repeatedly cranked the machine in a selection of records as varied as English weather. Popular classics such as "Cavalleria Rusticana" and "Poet and Peasant" might be followed by a hit of the day —"I'm forever blowing bubbles" or "Broken Doll", for instance — then, for Grandad's benefit, Tom Foy, the Yorkshire comedian or, especially for both grandparents, one of Harry Lauder's. These gramophone recitals always included an obligatory item for Grandma: "Where my Caravan has rested", sung by Peter Dawson. A song, maybe a touch sentimental, that somehow summed up for her the long past struggles to reach this later day's comparative calm as our matriarchal head. A large cardboard box beneath the bamboo table housed the records. Many bore the "Winner" label on which an intriguing picture showed a jockey passing a winning post with neither he nor his mount in need of reins, as he held aloft a gramophone record in each hand. This feat impressed in much the same way as did Douglas Fairbanks' athletic stunts at the cinema.

Large pictures looked down on the crowded Room. A full length daguerreotype of Grandma's parents taken in their Mansfield backyard. He in frockcoat, upper lip clean shaven and a narrow jawbone beard in Abraham Lincoln style. She, crinkly hair unflecked by grey but a drawn face showing she possessed few teeth, in a bombazine skirt full as an inflated balloon. A thick-length picture of Grandma's brother, Uncle Jim, also monochrome, proud in the uniform of a Northumberland Fusiliers' sergeant. He was killed in action at the Modder river engagement during the Boer War. A coloured study of a young Grandad, recognisable facially yet unfamiliar because of the shock of black hair. A long frame above the chiffonier holding three Lincoln views: cathedral, castle and Newport Arch. And a pen and ink drawing of the Grand Canal, Venice, the work of my late father, hung near to the lamp bracket.

No changes in the Room's lay out occurred during the decade nor, indeed, during the next (the last of the family's tenure). Everything was the same with the addition of one new item — a small bookcase acquired circa 1934 and somehow wedged beside the piano.

Nobody even considered any alterations.

Prudent housekeepng was demonstrated by our full coalhouse and, I later realised, in the Kitchen (as the living room was called). Hearth-rugs were put together by pegging on to stout sacking snippets of cast off worsted jackets, trousers and skirts. The resulting random and variegated pattern of greys, blues and browns, herring-bone, stripe and plain, was not unpleasing and, more to the point, wore well. White pointed ends to our yellowy window curtains were crocheted by Grandma. In odd moments she twisted old newspaper into spills which were placed on the mantelpiece in a china ornament made specifically to hold them. These were handy for fire lighting and, on occasion, coaxing dabs of sweet nitre into a paining hollow tooth. The ornament, a bobble-hatted small girl leaning over a pond fence feeding a duck, now resides amid an array of assorted bric-a-brac in my own home, its power to transport one back over the years strong.

The mantlepiece's main item, though, was a white china dog squatting on its haunches and placed precisely central. The dog fronted a wall mirror and when seated at table in certain positions a reflected arched back could be seen in addition to its placid — and, to my way of thinking, smug — face. It had been given to Grandma ages before by one, Aunt Price (not Mrs. or Miss Price you will note), a lady long deceased but still revered, whose memory was forever green. From grown-up reminiscence I gradually built up a mental picture of Aunt Price: tall, thin, grey, leg-of-mutton sleeved and immensely wise. Correct or not, the impression could not be checked as no photograph of the lady survived. Any idea of the china dog being broken or even slightly chipped was too awful to dwell upon. Fortunately it survives in unsullied entirety, a cousin its present custodian.

Of the Kitchen's large pictures, that of Queen Victoria — "the old Queen" in grandparents' parlance — dominated. The picture was a famous one repeated in countless working-class homes: nearly in profile, wearing a white glengarry-shaped cap with rear ribbons, one pudgy hand cupping her chin, the other holding an open book. Really the pose was as stiff and unnatural as any in our family album. When you came to think about it, the Queen's portrait was from an era only thirty years past yet wildly different in ethos from our 'Twenties. "What would the old Queen have thought?", Grandma sometimes enquired to no-one in particular. We knew what she meant. An omnibus query taking in not only the immediate subject but also girls' cropped heads and short skirts, women smoking in public (even in our town), the (to her) strange sounds of the Savoy Orpheans and other dance bands issuing from wireless loudspeakers.

As in other old houses, our Kitchen was always warm in the coldest weather, turning in short time numbed feet and fingers first to 'hot ache' and then normality. This happy quality did not wholly come about by the fact no door opened directly to outdoors, nor the fire's splendid capacity to throw out heat. (A good example of utilitarian looks concealing functional near-perfection). Each October Grandma retrieved from a dresser drawer two long curtains of blanket thickness. One, a draw-curtain clerical grey in colour, screened the Back Kitchen door. The other, in contrast a cheerful autumnal yellowy brown, performed a like service for the entrance door. Both curtains at the outset gave strong evidence of six months' contact with camphor balls, but this was a small price to pay.

There were two more doors, at the foot of the stairs and to a space under them known as the Cupboard. I seemed over a period to acquire the latter by prescription, rather like a houseolder acquiring an easement of light. This started with banishments from the hearth-rug and finding my small form could fit into the Cupboard's entrance and still enjoy the fire's warmth. Also that the space under the stairs could nicely accommodate a stack of reading matter. The Cupboard was partly of standing height. Flush with the rear wall and below shelves of home made preserves was a wooden freestanding cupboard on whose top shelf were two much used volumes: a dictionary and a rather dated Pears' Encyclopaedia in addition to oddments such as Old Moore's Almanac and several editions of the local paper's yellow covered annual compendium. Dictionary and encyclopaedia were often consulted by Grandma in response to my queries and her own keen thirst for knowledge.

When the houses (or, more accurately, cottages) were built around 1830, the owner had obviously been a believer in fair shares. The garden land in front was divided into three uniform portions with neat grass paths between them. A smaller stretch between end house and the eastern boundary was similarly trisected. And a brick and pantile pigsty, tucked in the north-east corner, contained three equal compartments.

In season Grandad tended our two plots, his main sessions being Saturday afternoons, working off the combined effects of a sizeable dinner and pre-dinner Cross Keys beer. My infantile attempts to assist him with a small wooden seaside spade were not welcomed. Probably Grandad wished to brood undisturbed over his usual verbal defeat regarding the connection between Cross Keys patronage and belated meals. Not that a slanging match developed. Grandma, as injured party, pithily made her displeasure plain. Grandad, as guilty party, gruffly volunteered a few defensive replies. So in the garden on these Saturday afternoons he would tetchily say "Tek' yer 'ook". And I would watch his operations from afar, having taken the wooden spade away if not that mysterious hook about which it appeared best not to enquire. I, too, then felt hard done by; the more so because, if Grandad had but known it, my sympathies were on his side. (In such manner, even at three or four years of age, are battle lines drawn in the war of the sexes).

Around 1922 the easternmost large strip was detached from the tenancy of the eastern end house because the new tenant, a widow, could not work it. So Mr. Blades from down the road rented it, setting a new standard for Grandad and Mr. Cooper to aim at. In no time, it seemed, the newcomer's strip presented an aspect of potato plants hilled in regimental lines, virile kidney bean shoots twisting their way round plot-wide frames, pea shoots, twining up an immaculately straight row of crossed sticks and the several varieties of cabbage in trim formation. Mr. Wilkinson, our nearest professional, could hardly have bettered the crop either in appearance or fecundity. Then, after two or three years, Mr. Blades arranged with his landlady (Grandma) for a change to be made. Gone were the ordered rows of potatoes, peas, beans and cabbages and in their place a flattened expanse bordered and divided into sections by high, wide-meshed, thin-gauge wire, each section with a prefabricated hen house. Mr. Blades had gone into poultry keeping. Accordingly our awakenings now coincided with cock crowings, home leavings and returns with a chorus of cluckings. Mr. Blades' visits were now twice daily; light grey working clothes made a shade lighter by flour (he was a baker by vocation), bucket of chicken meal nicely balanced on cycle handlebars. A quiet, worthy, kindly man.

With so much space taken up by gardens and chickens little remained for juvenile games. In fact it was limited to the path leading from the gate and a length of some thirty feet at the back between our bike shed and Mr. Cooper's shed, flattered by the name 'Yard'. The path, running parallel with our western boundary, had drawbacks. Half its length had a pronounced gradient and any improvised cricket and football games were further bedevilled by a ball's proneness to go either into a fearsomely thorned hedge or Mr. Cooper's garden. The so-called yard, therefore, usually provided the arena when sundry grandchildren, nephews and nieces descended upon the three households. Best of all were hockey matches, played with walking sticks. Girls were not inhibited as in football, and the confined pitch occupied by seven or eight milling

43

juveniles staged some stirring contests, dispelling the quiet of many a holiday afternoon.

In those early 1920s the three divisions of the pigsty had different employments. At one end — nominally the widow's — it was quite empty. The other end served as a hen house for Mr. Cooper, its door encircled by a tangle of meshed wire. This rough enclosure held a special fascination. A Cooper grown-up daughter, temporarily living with her parents, 'had a way' with animals and birds. She trained two chickens to answer to the names of Brownie and Beakie, and, on the word of command, scurry to her feeding hand. Even more impressive, she got the more dexterous Beakie to fly on to her shoulder. "Better than a circus act," Grandma said, to the general agreement of everyone. Grandad's part of the pigsty contained just one object, but a considerable one: a Lincolnshire wheelbarrow, a species deserving of some explanation.

Regarding things Lincolnshire, the wheelbarrow is not perhaps so deserving of fame as the county's jolly and tuneful Poacher song, but it surely should not be ranked lower than, say, the ancient Lincoln-green cloth. Up to the 1950s the wheelbarrow remained a utilitarian object though not under estimated as a workman's necessary implement. Later, with the arrival of more affluent times, it turned also into a prized example of olde worlde craftsmanship worthy to serve as stationary display platform for the bourgeoisie's choice plants. And even to achieve the dignity of a permanent place in Lincolnshire rural craft museums. An upgrading in status came too from scarcity value caused by the dwindling pool of craftsmen.

For a true Lincolnshire wheelbarrow was born of a happy union between skilled wheelwrights and blacksmiths from the making of 'hales' (Handles) to the welding of tyres. Its construction closely followed that of a farm cart, including oak spindles turned by a hand tool and boards secured with special 'hand clench' nails. Every joint was painted with red lead paint and the finished barrow was painted orangey red with black ironwork, the traditional colours.

The specimen that graced our pigsty embodied all these traditional facets except — heresy of heresies! — it had been repainted battleship grey. But to me its very size made up for any departure from colour customs: handles so far apart my immature arms were fully stretched when trundling, so heavy my puny strength hardly enough to trundle even when unloaded. Grandad could shift a heap of manure on to its ample boards in one loading.

One could no more imagine wash day not taking place on Monday than Christmas occurring in March. Somehow day and event were immutably entwined. Tradition had much to do with it and perhaps a touch of puritan penance too, decreeing that after a weekend of comparative relaxation the week's first working day should tax housewives' endurance. Of course the Monday wash day tradition still holds but latter day housewives tend to be less rigid and, with their electrical labour saving devices and less bulky articles, have not the work their 'Twenties predecessors had.

Then preliminaries started before breakfast with the lighting of a fire under the brick-enclosed copper. After the meal three necessary items — washtub, dolly and dolly tub — were placed in position near to wicker clothes-baskets piled high with the week's wash. The massive mangle was already there. It, together with the dresser which had been moved from the living room to accommodate a newly acquired wireless and its table, dominated the brick floored back kitchen. By the time our washerwoman arrived the stage was set. (Grandma had a weak heart and this hired help represented her sole concession to infirmity).

The washerwoman possessed the most redoubtable forearms I have ever seen on a woman. Before long the back kitchen filled with steam so dense the pantry door could scarcely be discerned. It was a fascinating scene. The washerwoman working doggedly at washtub and dolly tub, suds glistening on her mighty arms, talking continuously. It amounted almost to a monologue, a hovering Grandma supplying but an occasional comment for the flow to go on. Her successful son, so much more accomplished than her other offspring, what her gardener husband had to put up with from his employer and so on; the stuff of a mature married woman's life.

Mid-morning and a break for 'lunch' (the coining of the word 'Elevenses' was a generation away). Lunch, too, in this instance involved more than a modern elevenses' hot drink and a biscuit. Here great steaming cups of cocoa were drunk, hunks of thick bread and cheddar cheese and currant pasties consumed. (I suspect the pasties were baked with our washerwoman in view). Thus fortified, the prospect of the cold remains of a weekend joint did not seem too bad.

The washerwoman temporarily lost her audience soon afterwards when the insurance man arrived. His Monday morning visits had the inevitability of the day's cold meat dinner. About 11 a.m. he could be seen at the gate sedately dismounting from his bicycle, unstrapping from his carrier a worn Gladstone bag and making his way in due solemnity to our front door. Undeniably he had a presence, a presence unimpaired by a cycling dress of Norfolk jacket and breeches. He had the knack of apparently giving weighty judgements while act-

Grandad and Grandma circa 1932.

"The ornament, a bobble-hatted small girl leaning over a pond fence feeding a duck..."
(The duck unfortunately decapitated in the passage of time).

Family group circa 1923 (The hole in the hedge by the disused pump was my handiwork and gave access to the forbidden Field).

ually saying very little. In this the removing of spectacles, sucking the end of one ear-piece reflectively and allowing a pause to elapse before saying "yes" or "no" or "perhaps" or even "um" were common ploys. Then another pause until saying, for example, "Well, if you increase the weekly payment to ..." He seldom addressed small boys so a lesson in seeming omniscience and a large spot on his left cheekbone could be taken in without hindrance.

The washerwoman departed after dinner. Long lines of sheets and garments pegged out before the meal to flap and billow were brought in. In readiness the fire had been stoked up, dampers adjusted, two irons placed on a bar hooked to the fire bars, an old half blanket with sheet on top spread on the Kitchen table. Grandma could then start an afternoon of ironing, taking one iron and using until cool and then turning to the other, working as steadily as Mr. Wilkinson down the road digging a garden. Judging from faraway eyes her thoughts were distant ones. Only an occasional slight noise from the fire, the rubbing of a warm iron on cloth and perhaps my turning a page or moving a toy disturbed the silence of those Monday afternoons on school holidays.

Naturally we and the neighbours called the nearest field *the* field because it adjoined our houses. Actually it was the first enclosure of a long grassland expanse undulating northwards to the Low Toynton Road. On this you were able to espy a whitewashed gable-to-road cottage and, at lower level a little further on, the whole length of a road bridge spanning the town-bound River Waring. After a Nottingham holiday in 1923 I was apt to imagine this bridge as a stationary open-top tramcar with the evenly spaced gaps between its uprights as the windows. In such wise did a rural child retain a happy urban memory.

Ownership of the field went with a detached house which bordered it. In my earliest days the occupiers were the Woodwards, a quite bewildering family. In addition to Mr. and Mrs. Woodward there were seven offspring, four male and three female. In descending order of age they answered to the names of Horace, Jack, Sunderby, Brant, Joyce, Ralph (known as Bubbles) and Monica. The first three were adults, Brant was near school leaving age. Then came a gap of around eight years to Joyce, with Bubbles not yet at school and Monica scarcely past babyhood. About quarter of a century separated oldest and youngest. Horace, indeed, looked considerably older than his actual years, being prematurely grey. Rumour said that long before he had fallen, or been thrown, into a bed of nettles and shock had grizzled his hair. (An interesting story but dubious, one feels). Our relations with the Woodwards were sometimes strained. For instance, I once arrived home blubbering from some hurt inflicted by Brant and straightaway hauled back by Grandma to face Mrs. Woodward. Formidable in such confrontations, Grandma won the day with Mrs. Woodward at first pugnacious but finally contrite. But, of course, for me there remained an aftermath of sly sallies from Joyce (in a class higher at infants school) and threats from an unrepentant Brant. Another rift long remembered occurred when Mother and I visited the Woodwards one summer evening. While she was talking to Mrs. Woodward, Bubbles (whom I had probably goaded) hit me on the forehead with a skittle. The immediately resulting egg-size bump caused a break in relations of lengthy duration.

The Woodwards moved before I was very much older, leaving as evidence of their tenancy a war-surplus Army hut which had supplied necessary extra sleeping accommodation. Their successors were the Wilkinsons, a middle aged couple with a grown up son. Mr. Wilkinson, like Mr. Woodward a gardener, and his wife were a worthy couple whose life revolved around unremitting labour. People came to say Mr. Wilkinson was a proven first-rate gardener. One could quite believe it. To see him in the mundane act of digging, for example — a tireless performance, spade contacting ground at perfectly spaced intervals, each near-spadeful turning over a similar quantity of soil, action rhythmic as a metronome — was really a study in professional competence. As for Mrs. Wilkinson, whenever you called she would be at work sternly scrubbing, purposefully polishing, intent on beating some mixture in a pudding bowl. What were their relaxations, I wonder? They seemed to be an English equivalent of the continental peasant: thrifty, hard working, respectable.

The Wilkinsons soon made it plain the passage of small boys across the field ("*their* field"!) would incur displeasure. This was awkward. Their living room window commanded a sweeping prospect of the field. But this was partly impeded by the ex-Army hut and a trio of horse chestnut trees grouped in the in the field's centre also helped. So only the first part of a dash held risk. And towards midsummer before falling to the haymakers, tall grass nearly concealed my small form when bent double. The field beyond, my beloved Crooks, was therefore enjoyed as frequently as before the Wilkinsons arrived.

"Y' watch out for owd Tommy Waller!", said the big boys from down the road on discovering my habit of scampering across the field to the Crooks.

They proceeded to vividly paint Owd Tommy's capacity to chase, chastise and —ultimate weapon — get one "summonsed". It appeared entering Waller territory involved something called trespassin', a sin provoking a summons which in turn led to police court, probably gaol sentence and certain disgrace. Such a dire chain of events prompted my mind's eye to envisage an all-seeing, telepathic monster scarcely human in form. Quite wrongly, of course. Owd Tommy turned out to be a thin, frail and elderly wearer of tinted spectacles whose cloth leggings hinted of some connection with 'the land'. Possibly years before he had been a quick moving custodian of a domain he was determined to keep boy-free, and acquired a fame handed down to such purpose it still lived. Or maybe big boys were merely carrying out their age-old custom of trying to scare small boys. At any rate, Owd Tommy and I never clashed and plainly he did not pose the threat of the Low Toynton farmer who owned several meadows up the road. This worthy would drive his pony and trap right into a meadow and was not averse to flicking his whip in the direction of any juvenile invader besides loosing the rough edge of his tongue.

But even before its dispelling, the spectre of Owd Tommy did not for long keep me away from the Crooks, so strong was its lure. Its very size captivated — acres and acres stretching northwards to within a field of the Low Toynton Road bridge, the north-east corner within hailing distance of the village rectory. Arriving from the other (home) end, the Crooks's joys were at once available. After negotiating a defending barbed-wired fence you swooped down an incline to a brook that in spate babbled as if aware Tennyson's Somersby brook was but a few miles distant. My brook emptied itself into the Waring whose bank was an especial delight. At its highest point crumbling chalk had left a ledge just wide enough to take a boy's feet and dangerous enough for him to identify when using it with an exploit from the local cinema's current matinée serial.

If you followed the brook's sedgy course to where it gushed into the Crooks, happily and squelchily sinking into borderng turf, there was another, if passive, delight. A big old dying willow leaned over the brook's entering, the uppermost part of its trunk gone leaving a shell, which might have been scooped out manually so even was the remaining wood. Ideal this shell for watching the abundant wild life unaware of a human presence — hares, rabbits, the many species of birds. I remember especially the antics of magpies strutting unconcerned round the ash tree that stood in isolation fifty yards away.

Truly my 'magic garden'. And not only mine for several of my peers were equally enchanted. We would dam the brook, splash in the resulting pool, search riverside grass for moorhens' eggs, fish for minnows, watch Buck Shaw catch eels from the deep spot just beyond the river bend and so many other things.

Often I debated where its strange title, the Crooks, came from. Nobody knew. Could it be from crooked trees? But the ash and the willow were the only significant trees in all this space. Two generations later an old lady, not hitherto consulted, told me. The field had once belonged to a man named Crooks.

Besides immediate neighbours and the Woodwards, occupants of houses westwards towards the first bend were familiar long before schooldays. All seemed inordinately old (but to the very young youths of sixteen appear old). Some, however, were indubitably so. Just past the Woodwards lived an elderly couple, Mr. and Mrs. Hall. Behind belted long net curtains and Venetian blinds (curtains *and* blinds were then common) they lived troubling nobody, a pair of ancients self-sufficient as two safely burrowed moles. Much more interesting, though, were the Dennises. They kept a market garden whose numerous fruit trees and several greenhouses obscured their old pantiled cottage. The approach, down a long side path darkened by a high wall and overhanging boughs, seemed mysterious and ominous. Then happily, the long path ended to reveal the cottage snug as a sleeping cat in tall grass. And Mrs. Dennis would often be sitting outside, bowl on knee shelling peas or peeling potatoes or slicing kidney beans, her hair severely middle parted, eyes behind wire-framed spectacles intent on her work. She would break off at once and shout for Mr. Dennis, who would let me accompany him to his greenhouses which were all so lengthy I should assuredly have got lost alone. He would pull on a Woodbine while he plucked our tomatoes with gnarled fingers, and ask when I should be starting school and weren't his tomatoes big? So we would return to his cottage to find Mrs. Dennis (now standing and showing her thick black skirt was almost ground length) and my escorting grown-up deep in woman talk. Mrs. Dennis always rewarded me with a luscious plum or pear and the way back up that forbidding path did not feel so sinister.

Mrs. Chapman could be classified as an immediate neighbour. She lived at "The Laurels", the town's last house going east (ours was last but two), and was a quiet elderly widow invariably dressed in tweeds. Mrs. Chapman lived alone with Laddie, a weighty terrier advanced in years. His mistress took him for short daily walks until even this gentle exercising proved too much. After this he contentedly slept near "The Laurels" gate, varying routine by amiably ambling a myopic thirty yards to our gate to be patted. To the end he was known as Laddie Chapman as if a human.

Square on the road's first bend stood a detached house everybody called the Hospital House. Here were sent patients suffering from infectious ailments such as scarlet fever. At odd times relatives could be seen at the French windows which overlooked the road, holding restricted converse with inmates. A rather depressing, if necessary, building one felt, redeemed by Mr. Horner, husband of the nurse in residence. Tommy Horner was interesting on two accounts. Firstly that surname — could he possibly be related to the famous Jack Horner who stood in a corner and who appeared so memorably in my nursery rhymes book? And secondly, a romantic past. He moved about awkwardly on crutches, small and thin and gaunt. Yet this broken frame carried an aura because he had been a jockey, and, it was said, he owed his present state to a riding accident. Though difficult to imagine Tommy on a horse and impossible to imagine him performing in the manner of the jockey on our Winner gramophone label, there lingered that suggestion of former daring deeds.

A little later, with a daily trek to school, other characters living further towards town became familiar too. A white wiskered retired bootseller who pottered around his garden in a blue suit superior to most men's best. Two big boys, the Heath brothers, who signalled to cronies by means of a cry similar to Johnny Weissmuller's Tarzan whoop in movies a decade later. An emaciated young man, unfit to work, spending his day wandering collar- and tie-less to lean over his front gate for brief spells. His stepfather, a workmate of Grandad's, a burly man seeming even more brawny and upright in contrast, who would greet one in thick Scots' brogue. The two little unmarried sisters ("No wi'out a bit, them — they keep a livin'-in maid!") scuttling across the road to their chickens, for all the world like the birds they were en route to feed.

FIVE : WILLINGLY TO SCHOOL

The town owned two elementary schools, Church of England and Wesleyan. When the time arrived for enrolment in one or other it is beyond imagining that any debate took place as to which I should attend. A Methodist family of several generations standing did not as a rule change allegiance.

The School stood beside the lesser of our two rivers (or, more accurately, an extended section labelled "The Canal" on old photographs), a pile tucked around a road bend, a mere fifteen years old and still raw-looking. Thin spiked iron railings bounded it for most of the way, matching those across the road that fenced off the river, then a high brick wall completed the boundary. Behind this wall stretched a woodyard, invisible when in school confines but whose steam-driven saw's intermittent wails, up to crescendo and down to diminuendo, punctuated playtimes and lessons like an ever-present banshee. Over the road opposite the bend a narrow footbridge spanned the river, innocent looking but in winter of sinister import. In snowy weather enemy Church School boys ("church humbugs") would steal, Red Indian fashion, through the churchyard and between the thatched houses lining St. Mary's Square, thus reaching the footbridge. A raking snowball fusillade followed accompanied by whoops and catcalls concerning "Wesleyan Swilltubs". If the position was not stoutly defended our boys' entrance itself could be stormed. On the other hand, a stout defence might develop into an offensive and insulting Swilltub taunts suitably avenged.

The Infants Department occupied two classrooms at the School's southern end which were divided by a folding glass-panelled screen. It was ceiling high and could be moved to and fro at will along upper and floor tracks, thus enabling one large room to be evolved for joint class activities. Such activities occurred at early morning assembly or when cavorting round the tiny desks and in the aisles between them, a continuous Indian file supposedly marching in time to the piano. Also on Christmas term's breaking-up when we sang seasonal hymns (quaveringly thin voiced as a flock of fledglings) and were packed off home with much good will, an orange and a little bag of sweets. The gifts were prized the more because only the infants received them although the sweets, if clutched in a warm palm, quickly assumed the consistency of a concreting matrix.

The younger class, five-year-olds, had the luxury of two teachers. Stocky, rosy cheeked Miss Winifred Achurch, who wore pince-nez anchored to one ear by a droopy golden chain, surely and benignly introduced small charges into a new world. Her pupil teacher assistant, Miss Greenfield, long black curls fashionably be-ribboned and a local beauty, we also liked. Later on her renown increased still more on marrying that archetypal folk hero, a professional footballer.

We were happy — that unreasoning, totally unqualified, carefree happiness small children attain. Infants' boys used the girls' playground. There we ran tirelessly, a pack of exuberantly yelling midgets, dodging among the big girls' skipping trios, hopscotch games and chattering groups, only momentarily piqued that the fleetest among us was a girl. In class we moulded plasticine, listened to stories, whispered, asked to leave the room, drew houses with impossibly angled cables and learned alphabet and rudimentary spelling by rote. A-B-C-D-E-F-G, C-A-T cat, D-O-G dog we chanted in singsong monotone, insistent liturgies furrowing minds like ploughs through soft soil. Rote is a method discredited by later educationists. Interestingly, the School at the time had no cases of dyslexia.

The following year, transferred to the other room to compose the new six-year-olds' class, we felt a perceptible tightening of discipline. Miss Tait, head of the Infants' Department, became our mentor. Within a few years of retirement, she had, likely as not, taught our parents, uncles and aunts, and so carried a mental dossier of earlier family failings. Miss Tait was quite urbane for much of the time but asperity could and did break out. Then the frowning brow seemed to be made more ominous by its halo of wispy grey air. "Hold out your hand," she would bark, and administer a cut with a grained stick that was about eight inches long. One's palm stung for a long time afterwards.

But the tenor of existence remained blithe inside the classroom and out. Our chants increased in scope to include minor multiplication tables; we read and wrote two-syllable words; learned about pounds, shillings, pence, ha'pennies and farthings; learned to sing unaccompanied after an initial tuning-fork note; made simple incursions into botany (known as nature lessons), hence the cleansed jars containing hips and haws, catkins and sticky buds which in season adorned the long windowsill. There were lessons outside in the playground called 'Drill' where we stood in columns doing exercises to the commands of "Hands above your heads", "Hands touching shoulders", "Hands down" and the rest. And on Wednesday afternoons we were taught 'to read the clock'.

Telling the time was a favourite lesson. The blackboard was removed, a large clock face with movable hands tied to the easel and each child summoned singly.

"Mary Boswell", Miss Tait might call, "ten minutes to four".

And Mary Boswell, a small auburn haired beauty, whose hazel eyes even at six made your knees like jelly, tripped to the front and pointed the clock hands accordingly.

Besides there being no dyslexia cases, everyone could tell the time long before reaching Standard 1.

Though a year seemed unconscionably long it passed and the annual move to a new class arrived. The greatest change came at age seven when Standard 1 and, incidentally, the Big School claimed us. The classroom initiation proved gentle enough. Our new mistress, another Miss Achurch, had as amiable a disposition as her sister Winifred of the Infants' Department. Her classroom, remembered now for the odd reason it contained a framed ink drawing of Sir

Richard Grenville on the deck of the *Revenge*, turned out to be a refuge from other innovations Big School status brought.

These were two: playground and the Big Room. No longer did we share the larger L-shaped enclosure with two hundred girls. In September 1921, at the beginning of the school year, the boys of our class transferred to the other playground, an all-male preserve. This transfer may have been salutary but in the earliest days its noise and sheer arrant masculinity overwhelmed. We were truly the smallest fish in a big pond with the largest, aged fourteen or thereabouts, twice our age. These last, glamorously near wage-earning capacity, scarcely deigned to notice the existence of anyone below the age of twelve.

Time ended, as it does all things, the tribulations of being a small fish. New rites and customs assimilated, the playground's terrors diminished in a matter of weeks and had soon gone altogether. And we learned to use, if not necessarily to understand, a whole new vocabulary brought home not long before by demobbed servicemen. Not until my own service days, twenty years on, did I realise every known Anglo-Saxon swear word was in common use in that playground of the early 1920s.

At ten or eleven a seasoned veteran and, if not a big 'un, certainly not a little 'un, it was hardly credible there had ever been any terrors. Size, of course, was important. Every boy carried mentally a physical pecking order — who could 'hit' who. All knew how to inflict pain. A selection of methods: the half-nelson; the monkey shave (clenched knuckles rubbed distressingly hard around another's jaw bone); the bending back of a prone adversary's leg on to a fist positioned at the joint; fingers bent back unnaturally far; the tip of an adversary's index finger pressed hard against that finger's own base.

Yet bullying was not particularly rife. An unwritten playground rule, and one generally kept, laid down that a boy could fight only one of his own size. This did not prevent the infliction of a minor torture on a junior guilty, or thought to be guilty, of a slight to oneself. But it did ensure that in a serious fight — or 'scrap' at it was known — no contestant had to face outlandish odds.

Around 1925 we had a more or less undisputed champion, though he by no means emulated or even approached the excesses of a Flashman. He rarely interfered with those pursuing their own concerns and much of his playground time was spent in shadow boxing with Perry, a mild lad devoted to scientific aspects of the noble art. Our champion's victory over Horace Moore, an aggressive raggle-taggle gypsy boy often in the town, earned him a respectful, though temporary, popularity. We all relished his swaggering "I could ha' licked 'orace Moore wi' one 'and". But Nemesis came in the person of Jimmy from the Church School. Likeable Jimmy, besides this likeableness, had an insatiable appetite for fisticuffs and, having vanquished all rivals in his own territory, one day stood outside our boys' entrance issuing a challenge to the reigning bruiser. After the ensuing battle our outclassed champion never again enjoyed so high a reputation. The more so when a County Education Department re-arrangement brought an influx of hefty lads from neighbourhood village schools. However, we were not able to see the defeat in true perspective. In the 1930s Jimmy, then a tough professional boxer fighting

54

as Seaman Jim Lawlor, achieved the ranking of eighth best welter-weight in the world. Actually our man had not disgraced himself.

Fisticuffs and sadistic forms of pain infliction were fortunately not the only playground activities — they were the sole ever-present ones. The mass ball game, a hectic and rumbustious skirmish, though not indulged daily, knew no particular season. Any resemblance to organised soccer was restricted to there being two goals (the cloakroom and woodyard walls respectively) and the oblong shape of the 'pitch' (i.e. playground). (Oblong shaped, that is, save for an indentation at the woodyard end caused by the toilets. The latter were remarkable for a urinal possessing a common stall with a height thoughtfully gauged to cope with generations of boys competing "to see who could do it the highest"). No one every really opted out of the ball game. Even if not a dribbling fanatic showing off national Charlie Buchan skills and half immersed in other matters on the playground periphery, you still booted the ball if it came too near (towards which goal was immaterial). Wonderfully the ball — an old tennis ball or a rubber one of similar circumference called a sorbo — seldom if ever broke a window. It did, however, often go through or over the railings that bounded one playground side, to be illegally retrieved by the miscreant responsible or legally by the good natured retired postman, whose domain it was.

What anonymous authority decreed the precise times when shops displayed marbles or whips and tops? An academic question, perhaps, and certainly not one to cross a boy's mind. Yet, as if some instruction from on high was made, the playground asphalt would become dotted with small chalked circles. Or provide an amenable surface for the tireless whipping of a myriad of tops where for ages there had been none.

"Ha' yer seen the moggies in Browns' window?", a crony might ask (moggies was then the local slang word for marbles, not cats). If you had not made this vital inspection you inferred from his verdict ("they're alright") the marbles possessed a glassy distinction that enclosed a twisting, centrally embedded motif of several alluring colours. Browns' Bridge Street windows had to be inspected forthwith although one's current financial position and adequacy of marble stock might forbid a purchase. A small grimy linen bag containing the stock received a thorough inspection despite foreknowledge as to its make-up: a dozen or so glass alleys from the necks of mineral water bottles, rather fewer single-coloured orbs whose surfaces resembled polished stone and a few treasured specimens like those in Browns'.

Tops were in two forms: the prosaic squat tubby top that girls adopted too, and the dashing lean bodied type shaped like a toadstool. Naturally the latter were favoured by boys in much the same way as were dropped handlebar bikes over the straight. It was well named — the window breaker. Whipped by an expert it could be sent airborne for yards at a time, landing in a new position still gyrating perfectly. Whipped by an enthusiastic novice, too steep a projection sometimes caused a shattered window pane. Such risks, of course, were its charm: squat tops were for little 'uns and girls.

At times the aggregate number of cigarette cards — inevitably and succinctly called fag cards — carried about our persons must have been prodigious. Card production was at its peak. Every brand from the ten-for-fourpence gasper to top price silk cut issued them. This, coupled with a high adult male consumption, ensured a plentiful supply reached us. The cards had a splendid wideness of subject matter — "Ships' Badges", "Foreign Birds". "Miniatures", "Lucky Charms", "Natural History", "Gilbert and Sullivan", "Flowering Trees and Shrubs", "Racing Caricatures", "Characters from Dickens", "Old Furniture" and scores more. Swopping cards ('trying to get the set') had a lure equalling any other playground activity. Sets of cricketers and footballers were the most eagerly sought but Wills' "Do You Know?" devoted to chunks of information (e.g. Do you know what causes fog? What ancient lights are? Why the flying fish flies?) proved popular enough, running to three sets of fifty cards between 1922 and 1926 (and a belated fourth appeared in 1933). Cards required neither for collecting nor swopping were used in the cigarette card game, an activity restricted to the 'good weather' terms. Two players took part, kneeling four or five feet from a wall near to which several cards were strewn. Each player alternately flirted a card, the aim being to land it on a card near the wall. When this occurred the touched card was won by the successful flirter. Some boys developed a quite astonishing proficiency; the flirting card, held between index and big fingers which were pressed back into the palm, was released when these two fingers quickly flicked outwards and it skimmed through the air with a most satisfactory incisiveness.

No behest from a secret agency fixed the conker season, of course, the sole playground game season in nature's gift. In September, as ever, all horse chestnut trees would be climbed or pelted from ground level, each base turned into a litter of sticks, stones and spiky half-shells previously a conker's habitat. Windfalls also enlarged one's stock, and when this happened the uplifting of spirits was akin to a successful punter's. Likely conkers were examined with a critical eye for flaws. Sometimes the most promising were committed to the oven — always provided the custodian of that essential amenity was agreeable or, better still, absent. Whether or not baking made the conkers more redoubtable is debatable for many developed a fatal outer brittleness. At the same time, many champions had been baked originally. To bake or not to bake — a terribly hard decision! The answer came when the conker, carefully centrally holed and threaded with a length of stout string, was suspended for an opponent to do his worst, or if you yourself took first strike.

To a seven-year-old the Big Room really did appear big. In lesson time it catered for the three top classes and for Prayers first thing in the morning, when the whole Big School assembled. Then some three hundred souls crowded in, the domiciled classes at their own desks, the younger visitors in the midway space that separated Standard 5 from Standard 6 and 7, or down the long aisle between the girls' and boys' entrance doors. We were a motley throng, standing subdued and inhaling the unchanging school odour: that compound of chalk, school-mixed ink, young bodies and, not infrequently, rain soaked clothing.

The Big Room possessed one outstanding quality — light. Several tall windows on the external wall were supplemented by a long narrow one placed high at the boys' entrance (and fascinatingly operated by a looped cord four yards in length). The other long wall was punctuated by the internal windows of Standard 1, 3 and 4 classrooms, the Big Room thus benefiting also from the light their playground-facing windows emitted. And the Big Room's plain brick walls were whitewashed except for a painted dado. Small wonder the gaslights, perched on the extremities of elongated upturned-T brackets, came into use only on the darkest midwinter afternoons.

Sundry items relieved the walls' plainness. A faded map of the world on our facing wall; a framed 1914/18 Roll of Honour, beautifully wrought in ink, hung on one side opposite a monochrome Niagara Falls photograph; near the boys' door hung a small blackboard that recorded the week's morning and afternoon attendance totals as they evolved; cupboards were stationed near the Standard 5 and Standard 6/7 desks on whose flat tops reposed drawing lesson standbys — prisms, spheres and other white painted solids.

Procedure at Prayers scarcely altered over the years, even after Mr. Waymouth's ascent to the headmastership: a hymn, an eyes-closed intoning of the Lord's Prayer and the announcements. 'Announcements' was sometimes a misnomer, turning into a harangue on the shortcomings of an individual or individuals. Or a warning of dire consequences should anything go awry during an imminent visit from the Schools Inspector, an apparently all-powerful being who held the fate of every teacher and pupil in indifferent hands. And, most terrible of all, the tirade when something did go wrong during the Inspector's visit.

After playtime on the mornings of Armistice Days we assembled in the Big Room for a second time. The Roll of Honour then took on a different guise to that of a rather magnificent wall decoration as we were enjoined to remember the fallen. Although many of us had no personal recollections of the Great War — and an increasing number were in like case as the years went by — its shadow constantly invaded our consciousness. Adults' talk at home; the sight of one-legged prematurely grey men on crutches, the one-armed with vacant sleeve pinned across jacket front; the hacking, racking coughs and pallor of the gassed. At eleven o'clock the two minutes silence had an added poignancy because of its completeness. No shuffle, cough or rustle disturbed the Room's stillness; not a footstep, cart rumble nor car horn could be heard from outside.

Empire Day had an affinity with Armistice Day in that both celebrated deeply felt national attitudes. On that day, the 24th of May, an extended Prayers allowed for a recounting of the glories of empire. The conventional phrases rang out — "an Empire on which the sun never sets" and so on — the great names (Wolfe, Clive et al) touched upon, as was the fact that we, by inference the non-commissioned ranks and likely to remain so, were nonetheless fortunate inheritors. All these sentiments, if taken in, were swallowed whole, as we, now paraded outside, watched the Union Jack highered. After all, of this gathering no child could have had a developed sense of irony: we knew nothing of Third World aspirations, nothing about Britain's cheap food. Furthermore, our generation was weaned (rightly?) on the ideals of Rupert Brooke and Julian Grenfell. The disillusion that Siegfried Sassoon and Wilfred Owen revealed was imbibed much later.

Of all the Big Room assemblies one stands out with near total recall. It happened on a Monday morning early in 1925. News reached us over the

The Wesleyan Day School in the 1970s when the building was being used as a youth club.

Pupils en route for school circa 1912.

Class occupying the far end of the Big Room circa 1910.

No. 4 Wesleyan Sunday School 1921

"There we are, nearly a hundred strong...".

weekend that Standard 5's teacher, Miss Simpson, had been killed while travelling to her parents' house in the Mablethorpe area. It is to be supposed she was an emancipated 1920s woman for she owned and rode the motorcycle which was involved in this fatal collision. Mr. Waymouth talked to us that March morning, briefly, eloquently and with fine delicacy, aware of what a shattered school could take. The playgrounds' clamour was muted all week. For most, you see, it was a first experience of personal bereavement. Nobody felt immortal any longer.

The Big Room's girls' entrance opened on to a space off which were two cloakrooms (girls' and infants') and the Teachers' Room. The space itself, partially occupied by superannuated long desks and, along the walls, glass-doored cases containing dusty objects of a vaguely scientific aspect, was tantamount to an additional classroom. Here, on elevation to Standard 6, was enacted the week's greatest trial. On Thursday afternoons Mr. Waymouth endeavoured to initiate us into the intricacies of square root calculation. The lesson would start off normally enough and then, when questioning showed many had understood little, Mr. Waymouth's ire rose. His voice grew louder and could stupefy brain and ears. Stupefaction, though, had to be fought in case you yourself caught that angry eye and received an unanswerable question. The relief felt on completing a square root lesson unscathed equalled that on getting an unexpected reprieve from visiting the dentist. Then a new timetable ended the shambles. Perhaps it brought relief to the teacher too.

The Teachers' Room attracted all the conjecture sketchily known and seldom visited territory is apt to do. What did the teachers talk about? How did the more human ones cope with she who screeched and trilled her way through the bedlam of a Standard 4 day? Answers or part answers to these questions came when in Miss Credland's class, Standard 3. Sometimes she would summon one to the Teachers' Room at playtime to request that her copy of *Teachers World* be collected from the newsagent's forthwith. A somewhat timorous entering of the sanctum did not prevent you noticing that the mistresses, so different from the commanding figures of the classroom, had an ease — apparently a bantering ease — with each other in the Teachers' Room. And that included the emotional mentor of Standard 4. Grown-ups were incomprehensible!

Each term the Teachers' Room served as a medical inspection room and it was during these sessions this 'out of bounds' spot became known to us. The doctor, after making stethoscope soundings, examined every child's scalp. These quests for lice earned him the irreverent title of "the Dick Catcher" and, though necessary, were resented by parents priding themselves on family cleanliness.

Girls were the Teachers' Room's most fequent visitors because another extra-curricular use was as a fitting room for the trying on of sundry garments run up by teachers and girls in needlework lessons. A monitor would be posted outside to keep boys away, the warning coming in usually explicit fashion. As for typical instance: "Y' can't go t' the Teachers Room cos Harriet

Pridson's tryin' on a new pair o' britches". 'Britches' was local patois for knickers, then, as ever, a staple source of playground humour.

The event occurred around midsummer on a Wednesday afternoon (to coincide with the shops' early closing day) and referred to in the local press as "The Annual School Treat of the Wesleyan Sunday and Day Schools". Which lengthy title did not imply needless reporters' verbiage but the official and strictly accurate one. For only roughly half the Day School pupils plus a few Grammar School pupils attended the Sunday School, where it was not unknown for a Church Day School child to belong (thus qualifying for Church and Wesleyan Treats). Like all notable childhood events, School Treat impressions are etched deep in memory. The whole day holiday; how anxiously eyes scanned rain threatening skies or, if actually wet, how the old adage "Rain before seven o'clock, clear before eleven" from jollying-up adults gave hope (and really did happen one year!); the noise and colour of the procession; high tea and the sports afterwards.

Memories have been reinforced by photographs taken at the 1921 Treat and a miraculously surviving newspaper cutting on the 1922 Treat. One of the 1921 shots bears the caption "Wesleyan Sunday School 1921" and shows its male half against a background of the Drill Hall end, which is in this setting as formidable as a liner's stern, and tall trees in full June foliage. There we are, nearly a hundred strong, closely huddled little 'uns squatting or kneeling, big 'uns standing behind packed just as closely. The moment is captured forever, faces half averted or shielded by raised hands from glaring facing sunshine, or frowning at the photographer under wide cap peaks and hat brims. What a miscellany of expressions not altogether caused by the sun —extrovertedly happy, introvertedly withdrawn, wishing to please, stolidly composed and, in one instance, petulant. Two lady teachers provide the sole female element. Expressions, however, are nothing numerically to varieties of attire. Here only short trousers appear general (though this is open to doubt for some big 'uns, legs obscured in the rear ranks, would probably be wearing 'longs'. Or the increasingly uncommon Edwardian knickerbockers buttoned at the knee). Besides the hatless there are all manner of cloth caps — junior versions of the male models — plain and striped round caps, limp narrow-brimmed sun bonnets, white and grey Panamas. Jerseys with and without collars, without buttons or buttoned at neck or shoulder and, apparently, in every imaginable shade of colour. There are examples of stiff best suits, striped and plain blazers, sailor suits, blouses, smocks, comfortably cool jacketless and jerseyless boys in white cricket shirts, their trousers encircled by popular snake-clasp belts, my cousin and I unique in velvet suits made the previous year for page boy duties at an aunt's wedding. Many are wearing ties including those of the then fashionable horizontal bar design and two bow ties are to be seen.

My 1922 newspaper cutting is not so immediately a reminder but it does confirm a half-remembered timetable, which never seemed to vary, as under:
... they (the mothers) handed them (the children) over to the care of the teachers outside the Wesleyan Chapel in Queen Street prompt at 2 o'clock.

Queen Street, a highly esteemed and normally quiet thoroughfare of solid

Victorian houses, would be awash with people long before 2 o'clock. The early arrivals formed a dense pavement-to-pavement mass facing the Chapel and its companion Sunday School, a mass broadening as later arrivals joined its fringes. It consisted mainly of mothers and unusually neat children shiny from recent aggressive scrubbing, but contained also bandsmen and members of the Boys' Brigade proud in their insignia.

Headed by the School banner, and accompanied by the Town Band, the children marched in procession to the Market Place ...

The emergence from the Sunday School of the senior Minister, his deputy, the Headmaster (Mr. Ogden), Mr. Waymouth (then the assistant master) and four prominent churchmen proclaimed action. The huge banner was unfurled, straddling the street and requiring six acolytes — one for each pole, four on the guide-ropes, the pole bearers' burden considerable. Behind the banner marched the blue uniformed Town Band whose rests from rendering the works of John Philip Sousa and the like were filled by the bugles and drums of the immediately following Boys' Brigade. Then came the competition entrants in fancy dress or wheeling decorated wheelbarrows and dolls' perambulators or carrying decorated hoops. Lastly the remaining children, a great straggling, somewhat self conscious, three hundred ambling two by two, class by class, flanking teachers amiably keeping some coherence to a wavering throng.

...to the Market Place, where songs were rendered by the poppy and fairy groups.

The halt served three purposes. Firstly it enabled poppies and fairies (groups of girls dressed accordingly, whose performance is my only Treat memory to have completely faded) to make public the fruits of much rehearsal. Nearly as important, going to the Market Place means the procession covered the main streets. Lastly, bandsmen rested lips and lungs, little 'uns their legs.

Then they proceeded to the Wong, watched by a large and interested crowd.

True enough, pavements along the route were thick with people engaged in the favourite Lincolnshire pursuit of standing and staring.

The Wong was the town's sports field, a name we never questioned but which must sound odd (and perhaps with oriental connotations) to non-locals. The word 'wong' or 'wang' is Anglo-Saxon and means a lord of the manor's southern field. It is well known throughout the county.

A large number of children were in fancy dress, and judging for the prizes took place immediately.

Not only the judging of fancy dress, for the little girls' decorated dolls' perambulators, small boys' wheelbarrows and hoops of both girls and boys came within the province of the lady judges also. Another 1921 photo assists here: eight decorated hoop winners, four white frocked girls, four boys standing behind, all blinking into strong sunshine with me, although markedly the smallest, agonisingly prominent in velvet suit and Panama hat (or so I felt at the time). The hoops are the real eye catchers, however, criss-crossed ingeniously with ribbons, foliage and flowers, Hilda Liney even spelling out her first name.

In 1922 fancy dress subjects ranged widely from topical "St. Dunstan's" to olde worlde "Old English Fair" and "Victorian Lady", from nursery rhyme characters ("Old Woman in a Shoe" and "Little Miss Muffit") to contemporary commercial ("Bird's Custard Powder", and "B.D.V. Cigarettes" and *Daily Chronicle*). There were callings — a Road Sweeper, an Admiral, a Newsboy, a Coster, a Monk and Fruit and Match sellers. There were Welsh and Dutch girls, conditions of mind and body ("Solemnity", "Fun" and "Fagged Out"), eatables ("Potatoes" and "Wedding Cake") and a non-eatable "Post Card Album". And a "Father Christmas", surely at midsummer as untopical as one could get, yet good enough to win 3rd prize in the boys' over-12 section.

The afternoon was devoted to games and then at 4.0 p.m. the children were formed up and marched down to the Sunday Schoolroom, where they sat down to an excellent tea ...

Games brought an outlet to energies pent up during the procession and the compulsory witnessing of Poppy and Fairy songstresses. Boys' best clothes soon rumpled and knees made grubby in the passports of release.

When breathless and in process of getting second wind, the Town Band in action could be closely savoured. Those worthies occupied a corner of the field, sitting on camp stools in a circle round their conductor. High collars undone, glossy-peaked hats tilted back, their wearers could perform informally. They had an air of knowing they had earned relaxation. The normally ruddy cheeks of one cornettist (a more familiar figure in a railwayman's uniform) were now positively crimson. The drummer, who had thwacked mightily the big bass drum strapped to his chest during the march, showing his spare frame's sinewy strength, could now sit at ease. The band drifted into a gentler repertoire of popular songs ("I'm forever blowing bubbles", "Peggy O'Neil", "Broken Doll") and musical comedy selections ("Maid of the Mountains", "Chu Chin Chow").

The 4.0 p.m. march to tea was a much less sedate affair than earlier. The marchers, now devoid of any Sunday-best feeling and given up to rich enjoyment, were thoughtfully taken by the nearest route avoiding main streets. Both Sunday School and adjoining Primrary School had been prepared to receive this descending horde. Long tables, created by planks on trestles, ran room length covered by snowy white table cloths. At the head of each table stood a ministering lady behind a massive steaming tea-urn. After grace we set to. Placed strategically down the centre of the tables were plates of provender: mounds of ham, tongue, jam, paste and cream cheese sandwiches, buttered scones and tea cakes, buns, sausage rolls and bilious looking cakes of a quite wonderful glutinous stickiness. On the boys' tables it was a matter of honour nothing, literally nothing, should be left uneaten. In pursuit of this worthy goal the mounds quickly disappeared amidst a deafening babble that restricted conversation to one's immediate neighbours. Some wild spirits would have a tea drinking competition in which impressive totals of ten and eleven cups would be consumed. The term "bun fight" must have been coined with feasts like this in mind!

After tea they again proceeded to the Wong, where games, sports etc. were held.

Which goes to show that many competitors in the aforesaid sports had digestions to rival a boa-constrictor's.

64

The sports were the Treat's most exciting feature. Two tracks were formed a little distance apart by parallel lines of hurdles ('trays' in local parlance), one for boys, the other for girls. Behind the hurdles lined the many spectators, whose cheers encouraged and laughter sometimes goaded contestants. Laughter because, besides straightforward athletic events, there were three-leg and sack races, where almighty purlers occurred, and egg and spoon races where disasters happened all the time. Over it all presided a (to his pupils) nearly unrecognisably benign Mr. Waymouth, resplendent in blue blazer, white flannels and straw boater.

The tracks, hemmed in by tightly packed spectators, seemed to give off a heightened scent of fresh June grass, a descending sun perceptibly lengthened shadows and every child hoped the Treat would not end for hours and hours and hours.

At 9 o'clock the children were again formed up, and a torchlight procession was headed by the Town Band... The procession marched to the Market Place, and after the singing of the National Anthem the children were handed into the care of their parents apparently tired out ...

Certainly we little 'uns were tired out but the torches, bobbing at the sides of our serpentine column, had a glamour which for the moment successfully fought off tiredness. After fluttering for some six hours over the Wong's entrance lashed to the gateposts, the banner could once again be espied well ahead, the Town Band following in its wake with an unimpaired volume. Soon the Market Place staged the Treat's final rite.

They were wonderful days.

SIX : THIS SPORTLING LIFE

The town's side-by-side sports fields, a semi-private Oaks Meadow and everybody's Wong, did not quite have a monopoly of transient events needing open space. Circuses, menageries and fairs usually found a temporary home on one of two inn paddocks (Black Swan or New Inn). Both were rather small but adequate for circus and menagerie tents and the truncated versions of fairs that showmen properietors condescended to send. Our fairs consisted of a steam roundabout, a manually operated children's roundabout and perhaps half a dozen sideshows including a coconut shy and hoop-la stall. The introduction of a dodgem car rink in the 1930s created a furore locally which really emphasised the limitations of our fairgrounds' attractions.

These infrequent travelling entertainments' apart, the sports fields staged most else of organised outdoor activity. And of the two the Wong, being a common, saw much the most. Besides Saturday and Wednesday mens' football matches, it served as sports field to both elementary schools, as venue for their school treats and for scratch games played after school and working hours by boys and youths.

Wong grasses had a toughness that withstood continuous pounding. Goal mouths were the only bare patches excepting for the diagonal footpath, south-east to north-west, that took in a corner of the official football pitch. A fortunate attribute, this tough grass, as the Wong had an area little more than two football pitches (the official one plus a no-man's-land to the northern boundary). This area was further reduced in 1925 when a newly created children's playground lopped off an appreciable segment in the south-west corner.

In the early 'Twenties the population's male half was mad about soccer. There were two mens' clubs, Town and Athletic, while the two elementary schools' and Grammar School's team places were coveted as if passports to sporting paradise. A cumbersome Grammar School adolescent could boastfully say to a group of Wesleyan School small fry "I'm first reserve full-back for the School." And, though his playing accomplishments were judged minimal and the statement greeted without comment to his face and with merriment behind his back, such was the game's prestige one could not help but be a little impressed.

Matters pertaining to Town and Athletic, however, brooked no levity whatsoever. At this time both were formidable as a glut of good players lived in the district, some of whom eventually turned professional. Except for one season the clubs competed in different leagues but could, and did, clash in cup tourneys. When this happened a contagion peculiar to males only spread throughout the locality affecting young and not-so-young in varying degrees. My symptons were a tingling sensation in the nape of the neck on first hearing about the forthcoming cup-tie, and a subsequent marked feeling that school's real purpose was a continuing playground argument on the teams' merits and demerits. A game between them shortly after the Great War became legendary. Preceeding season 1919/20 and billed as a practice match, a near riot developed. The *News* castigated both teams and apportioned blame equally. Fortunately later encounters did not result in a repetition although 'needle' could be guaranteed and were not for spectators of nervous disposition.

Local derbies formed the icing on our football cake but no Town or Athletic home match was without interest to big males and excitement to small. Excitement welled up as you mounted the flint-strewn gentle rise to the Wong's wide entrance gate. On one side stood an agricultural implement warehouse and a stretch of livestock pens, on the other the Black Swan whose long gable wall carried lurid posters of Moxon's and Sanger's circuses or Bostock & Wombwell's Menagerie ages after their visits. Of all our many pubs, the Black Swan being so sited had a singular appropriateness. Over its street entrance was a long board naming the licensee — "Frank Pattison, ex-Sunderland, Clapton Orient and Lincoln City". Appropriate indeed. And well beyond the Wong's gate you could see goal-posts, now diginified by match day nets, and a freshly marked out pitch that had been roped in.

These ropes, though, were respected by spectators only during the actual match. Before it a simple mass ritual, "shootin' in", took place. With several footballs available, two or three stout spirits risked decapitation while jointly keeping goal to a bombardment of shots from every conceivable angle and distance, those from very near getting suitable derision (e.g. "Another bluddy baby-liner from owd Bert!"). Shooting-in served the dual purpose of warming blood on chilly days and allowing budding sharpshooters and tyro custodians to show their mettle. And 'prentice full-backs too, for several such positioned themselves behind the goal returning the many off-target shots to the massed assembly in front. Eventually shooters-in would be joined by players and we knew the real business of the afternoon was imminent.

At half-time the crowd, except for emulating boys starting kickabouts behind the northern goal, gathered on the centre of the pitch. Favoured elders chatted to players while we little 'uns respectfully stared our fill, storing scraps of overheard talk for future use. Players sipped cups of steaming tea that had been poured from an immense metal jug, some additionally pulling on a cigarette. Neither tea drinking nor 'a quick drag' squared with advice from boys' papers. According to them, lemons should have been sucked and cigarettes avoided because of shortening one's wind. Still, this was real life and you never could account for the vagaries of grown-ups.

After a match everyone — spectators, players and officials all — spilled out from the Wong like sand grains from the top half of an upturned egg timer. South Street filled from side to side with a lengthening concourse that did not thin until the East Street junction hived off its quota of the homeward-bound. The street resounded with the tramp of a myriad pairs of feet and masculine voices from deepest bass to boy treble. And when a season was advanced, our visible steaming breath outdoing cigarette smoke, recently lit gaslamps gently illumined muddied gladiators and cloth capped spectators.

Above all was the feeling, dimly sensed and never voiced, that these physical encounters were the ultimate, the quintessence of enjoyment. Life could not possibly hold any greater rapture.

By 1926 the Athletic was in decline. They had left a superior Oaks Meadow and confined to Wednesday football on the Wong pitch used by the Town club on Saturdays — and everybody else at other times barring still-recognised Sabbaths. Their Saturday stars had joined the Town and they fielded a youngish side that included a speedy, sporting curate at outside-right and Grammar School teenagers. Actually this 1926 side was quite a fair one unfortunate in having to undergo comparison with notable predecessors of very recent memory.

But a comedown it undoubtedly was. The Oaks Meadow had echoed to supporters' cheers at these predecessors' deeds. This neat enclosure next to, and approached from, the Wong boasted a wooden grandstand, a proper 'box office' at the gate and enough high corrugated iron sheeting along the Wong boundary to prevent free viewing. The goal-posts had circular uprights — and thought mightily trendy — whose bases were painted black, a design to accord with the team's black and white vertical striped jerseys. Such, then, was the Athletic's home, one fit to compare with any small town ground in Lincolnshire. (One set of trendy goal-posts ended up on the Wong, placed off the playing pitch parallel to a touch-line, usefully serving for scratch kickabouts instead of the usual two piles of jackets).

The Athletic team fully matched its setting, reaching a peak in 1922 by winning two league championships (Wednesday and Saturday leagues) and three challenge trophies. It had strength from royal blue sweatered Charlie Bedlow or Len Cox (who shared goalkeeping duties) to its darting, tricky outside-left. And literal strength in full-back and centre-half positions. Sid captained the Athletic from left-back, a seasoned veteran possessing cunning, knowing precisely opponents' whereabouts at any particular juncture. He paced his game, believing in saving his legs, using stamina like a miser doling out sovereigns. Not for Sid a venturesome, tentative tackle: he waited until his adversary appeared slightly off balance or wavered or was too boxed in to pass the ball and then went in relentlessly. His capacity for snuffing out the threat of a fleet opponent never seemed more evident than in a local derby. How the Town supporters brayed and hooted and yelled "Foul!" and more personal rudenesses when Sid summarily dispossessed one of their favourites.

Sid's full-back partnership with Inky was famous. A complete contrast to the cool Sid, Inky had no qualms about committing himself in a tackle. Barrel-chested and with muscled thighs of tree trunk sturdiness, he could balloon the ball an extraordinary distance. No more fearsome sight than Inky bearing down on an opponent, whether grim or grinnning, was to be found in the whole county. At cente-half Tartar showed similarities: a hardness of tackle, an ability to match aggression. But there resemblance ended. Tartar, belying a biggish physique, could be as light on his feet as a ballet dancer, trapping the ball effortlessly, and gently flicking a pass to an unmarked colleague. Little wonder he caught the eye of a Sunderland scout.

Mentioned together, Buck and Chuck, inside-right and centre-forward, sounded like a music hall turn. Thin faced, smiling Buck with his little twinkling steps, long jersey almost covering shorts hitched high, forelock bobbing and hankerchief grasped in right hand, had craft not one wit behind that of the older Chuck. The latter, one of three renowned footballing brothers, black hair balding at the crown, thus looked from the rear like a tonsured monk. The pair loved goals as confirmed drinkers love their cups. In that memorable 1922 season they aggregated 98 between them, of which Buck scored 58 and Chuck 40.

Really there were two Athletic headquarters. The official Black Swan, in whose hospitable interior the committee met and home and visiting teams changed; and, unofficially, Sid's. Sid ran a barber's shop handily sited a few yards from the Town bridge. As has been noted, in a small place where everyone was known, warts and all, a barber's shop had a role far more significant than its counterpart in an anonymous city. As barbers' shops were then wholly male preserves, few subjects were taboo and discussion salted with less refined language. Naturally at Sid's talk tended to gravitate to Athletic matters. Committee members dropped in whether or not in quest of Sid's professional services. They seated themselves in the salon, going over the last match and looking forward to the next, the air blue with pipe and cigarette smoke. "Young Smarty Tilcock played a good ga'em", one might say and more, often "What d'you think, Sid?" And Sid would stare with greater concentration on the hair he was snipping or chin he was shaving, pause a moment, look up and deliver a judgement.

Sid's salon contained a reminder of Athletic's palmy days for years after the club folded — a large photogravure team portrait hanging between two mirrors. It drew eyes away from the fronting tiers of brilliantine bottles, shaving soaps and brushes and even people's own reflections. The group had been photographed in a goal mouth graced by those fashionable black-based uprights, the net acting as a backcloth. The players stood proudly, arms folded over chests. Men in their prime.

Very fittingly, Sid Pearson's shop stood a little way off one river bank opposite the Town club's Vine Tavern headquarters a little way off the other. It was a dark little inn made so by an overshadowing warehouse. Yet it held for we small boys an aura by reason of association. On the way home from Friday afternoon school we would look across river to see if the Tavern's bay window had been adorned by a team sheet. If it had we scampered over the Town bridge, athirst for news. These team sheets, provided by a sports goods firm, had eleven figures of footballers in pyramidal (and classical) formation: a goalkeeper, two full-backs, three halves and five forwards. On a dotted line under each figure a name would be written in Bish's neat handwriting. Inspecting Town team sheets was as compulsive an exercise as inspecting stills outside the cinema. We milled round the window like twittering sparrows round bread crumbs. All the same, well informed sparrows. "Jackie Foster is playin'," somebody might gleefully shout, voicing our corporate approval. Or sometimes disgustedly. For instance — "They've picked that useless Dorkins agen!"

For home games both teams changed at the Vine Tavern. They emerged in twos and threes to walk the two hundred yards over the bridge (which carried a match poster lashed to its railings), and along South Street to the Wong. They walked through knots of interested market day shoppers and dismounted errand boy cyclists, boot studs clicking on asphalt and cobblestone. All red jerseyed Town heroes were recognised and occasionally a doughty adversary too. Nigger Coatsworth, a swarthy inside-right who had teased many a Town defender in the cause of Lincoln Clayton's, strode among us familiar as local Tranner and Soapy. Very popular was Nigger, even with us partisan home team supporters. Indeed we thought him fit to swop his blue and white stripes for Town's red. It would have been hard to find a greater compliment.

The Town Football club went back to 1901 and Bish Laughton had been its secretary from the beginning. He received a County Football Association long service medal in 1920, a year which turned out to be a halfway mark for he still held the post when war broke out in 1939. In a very real sense Bish *was* the Town, the single constant factor in a period of nearly forty years. He had signed several hundred players during that time and seen many changes in the composition of his committee. Yet not so many as the long span might suggest: committee members served long and Bish inspired loyalty.

Bish, one of those local inexplicable nicknames that seemed to have originated in the mists of time, replaced a perfectly good Harry. Replaced, that is, for intimates of the football fraternity. Contemporaries such as Mother used Harry and juveniles respectfully (and rightly) addressed him as Mr. Laughton (just as we did Mr. Pearson). Whichever name used and whatever the age group of the person being talked to, he remained the same: kindly and somehow transmitting the feeling to youngsters their opinion counted. A warming and not too common a quality.

He had lost the use of his right leg when a young man and stumped around on crutches. On match days he and committee members manned the Wong's entrances. At half-time they betook themselves to a touch-line to watch the second half. Bish, with mackintosh open in all temperatures revealing a watch chain spanning waistcoat, hands thrust deep in pockets weighed down by spectators' entrance money — seemed as changeless a Saturday sight as the Hagworthingham carrier.

By trade he was a boot repairer and could daily be seen going to his little Foundry Street shop. Not for another decade could one see him in his other role as Vine tavern landlord, expansively at ease on a wooden settle, crutches propped beside him. Not all football's notabilities perform on the field of play.

A thought occurs that Bish might have been an abbreviation of Bishop. Somehow it doesn't seem all that inappropriate.

Generally speaking, of our two clubs Town had the edge, their sole reason for envy the few seasons of Athletic's Oaks Meadow tenancy. And to supporters, anyway, success on the field transcends ground appointments. In those heady early 'Twenties years, Wong crowds of 1500 were commonplace and a far greater multitude witnessed a match one dullish Wednesday afternoon in mid-autumn. Having made excellent progress in the stiffest competition entered, the Lincolnshire Senior Cup, the Town now faced professional opposition in Gainsborough Trinity. After prayers that morning, Mr. Waymouth gave notice in starkest terms of dreadful consequences for anyone cutting school. A notice, needless to say, unheeded by some. We of weaker fibre who did heed found afternoon school quite insufferably long. And on merciful release arrived at the Wong breathless to find a crowd so densely packed we, for the most part, saw the ball only when it was airborne. Completing our deprivation and discomfort, Gainsborough won 3—1 and the truants' verdict that Town were not disgraced did not mitigate feelings at all.

From 1919/20, when a league championship (with one just defeat) and two cups were won, the team reached a 1925 peak, winning in knock-out competition a record eight trophies. That 1924/25 season was unashamedly a pot-hunting campaign, leading players being 'saved' for cup-ties and league matches contested with weakened representation.

Naturally the 1924/25 cup haul attracted press attention, one writer describing Town as "one of the best amateur teams in the country". Here the word 'amateur' requires a little qualification, for two stalwart veterans had seen pre-war Lincoln City service while another had been with Tranmere Rovers a little earlier. And a purist might have pointed out that seven of the all-conquering eleven travelled here from Lincoln, twenty-two miles away, so the side was not strictly local. Anyway, the four really local players deserved parity with this imported talent. At wing-half Jimmy Carter and George Markham (of the previously mentioned 'three brothers') performed prodigies, Jimmy cogent in tackling, George cunning in distribution. Tranner ran fleetly at outside-right as did Soapy on the opposite wing. Soapy caught the eye of Grimsby Town and accordingly turned professional, like one of the younger Lincoln imports with his City club.

"Cum on the red 'Er ins," we piped and our elders yelled. The Red Herrings

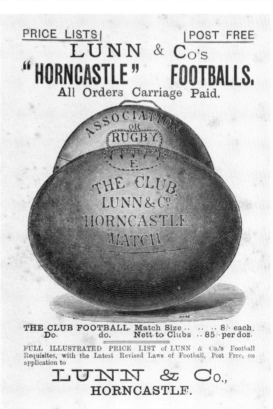

Advertisement: Alcock's Football Annual of 1884. It proves the town's leather industry had a nation-wide clientele.

71

Town FC circa 1924. (Players (left to right) back row: Carter, Dunne, Wild, Lusher,
Bullivant, George Markham; front row: Parker, Dovey, Groves, Parrish, George Smith.
'Bish' Laughton is on Markham's left. This line-up includes old professionals
in Wield and Dunne (Lincoln City) and Groves (Tranmere Rovers), while Dovey and Smith
were to sign professional for Lincoln and Grimsby Town respectively.

Cricket on the Oaks Meadow circa 1930.

Section of the crowd 1923.

Len Cox winning the 1924 Walk.

never obliged to greater effect than in vintage 1924/25.

One Saturday afternoon in the mid-1920s Town had a home fixture against Boston Town Reserves. The previous day's *News* gave the Town's line-up and went on to mention their opponents would be fielding a centre-forward who had but recently worn the colours of three Football League clubs, two of them in Division 2. Boston Town was a typical minor professional club, a refuge for old pros from the big time and a launching pad for young hopefuls desirous of catching the attention of a big club's scout. Its second string, Town's visitors, generally consisted of young hopefuls.

The afternoon turned out fine, crisply autumnal, an invigorating breeze chasing the few visible clouds. The usual thousand-odd crowd was lining the ropes when the teams kicked off. Boston looking trim and confident in light blue and white jerseys of Aston Villa design. We quickly picked out their centre-forward, a blond man of upright carriage. He differed from the customary ex-League pro in that he was far from being a veteran in years — around 28 at most.

Town soon gained an upper hand and a comfortable lead. The second half was the same, Boston's centre-forward making no headway whatsoever although his colleagues constantly played to him. The crowd, vocal and partisan as always, had made a few catcalls in his direction. In the second half these continued sporadically until a wag shouted:

"Why, 'e's onny a thotty bob man!"

Now "thotty" (broad Lincolnshire dialect for thirty) shillings was well below the minimum weekly wage any self-respecting grown labouring man would conceivably work for. Even a farm labourer — the wage upon which all local comparisons were based — got about thirty-six shillings. In other words, thirty was nothing short of insulting.

The 'thotty bob' taunt somehow caught the crowd's mood. It took up the cry, jeering as only a crowd can, secure in its knowledge of individual anonymity. The jeering went on whether the centre-forward was in contention or not, unmerciful and continuous — "Thotty bob man", "Thotty bob mab" — a cruel, monotonous refrain as remote from normal Lincolnshire tolerance as crabbed age from youth. The Boston player had but a brief year before been a League aristocrat. In that period he had descended to the second string of a Midland League side and a crowd's butt into the bargain.

It was my first experience of seeing a man metaphorically kicked when down.

In contrast to thriving winter soccer, no town cricket club existed to act as a summer counterpart until mid-decade. The schools, of course, played cricket. I recall Mr. Waymouth lecturing Standard 6 boys on the game. He faced us, sitting on the lid of a front row desk, one leg in the gangway, a relaxed pose in keeping with a sports subject discussed at playtime.

"Cricket", he had averred, "is the finest game ever invented because it is the one team game where each player has to rely on everyone else".

Personally I could not see that soccer made any fewer demands on teamwork (for the moment forgetting show-off individualists), but contrary opinions were not ventured to a Mr. Waymouth in full spate. Standard 6, an age mix ranging from possible grammar school material to near-14 year old huskies, supplied the nucleus of any Wesleyan School sporting representation, invariably from the husky faction.

That summer saw some lively contests against the Church humbugs. A Second XI also performed, made up of juvenile novices such as myself, who thrashed at every ball when batting and thought fielding both a bore and a chore. All our cricket was played on the Wong, where wickets were selected from the two grassiest patches which happened to be the legal distance of 22 yards apart. The resultant low scores owed as much to vagaries of bounce or non-bounce or other caprice on unsuitable turf as to opposing bowlers' skill. Nonetheless, one hundred and fifty or more boys, including the fortunate pupils on the Grammar School's own field, were playing organised cricket while adults had no opportunity unless they travelled outside the town.

By around 1926 the picture had changed completely. Several factors — which may be guessed at — brought this about. A wish to play on the part of grown-ups and the knowledge the town had not possessed a cricket club since pre-war days were doubtless among them. Before that 1926 summer, too, sports pages devoted much space to H. L. Collins's Australian touring side, thus arousing much cricketing interest. And, importantly and much more materially, the Oaks Meadow became available. The Athletic football club had commenced its slide from the pinnacle of a few years earlier, first with the loss of several good players and then the transfer from a well appointed Oaks Meadow to the plain and unadorned Wong. (By the late 'Twenties the Athletic was defunct).

In small communities voluntary organisations, sporting and otherwise, are apt to wax and wane and go out of existence. (They can also prove remarkably long lasting, like our Town F.C.). The cricket club was a classic example of lusty re-emergence. An Oaks Meadow transformed — a pavilion replacing the grandstand; wooden benches dotting the perimeter of a pitch spruced by much mowing and rolling; a conscripting of wives and other ladies to prepare and serve teas; a mass of would-be players from town and district. A mass to embarrass team selectors — in a numerical sense at least — in the filling of Wednesday and Saturday teams. A grand formal opening of the Oaks Meadow as a cricket ground took place, performed by a cricketing celebrity: Clem Hill, who had represented Australia in 49 Test Matches, 1897-1911. Such an upsurge of enthusiasm deserved a celebrity.

The enthusiasm of that mid-'Twenties revival could not go on but had sufficient impetus to last some years. Wednesday and Saturday XIs took shape, the first drawn from shopkeepers, shop assistants, bank clerks and office workers for whom Saturday was a full working day. On Saturdays schoolmasters and senior Grammar School boys comprised the backbone. And there were adaptable people like the farmer from Hameringham, the poultry farmer from Fulletby and a landed gentleman from Martin Hall who could generally arrange to play on both days. The last two were arrivals of the late 'Twenties when the number of players had diminished and it was advantageous to have people able to step in at short notice.

In the heady first years someone had the idea of meeting the natural desire of all would-be players to engage in real match play by forming a league. It sounds preposterous now — a little town with a population of three and a half thousand, perhaps four hundred males of playing age and perhaps only a quarter of those wishful of active participation. But a cricket league there was, and it briefly flourished. Half a dozen teams competed; Grammarians, the Railway and the *News* among them. No matter there were as many grey- as white-trousered performers, that bowlers were so dominant totals of under 40 runs were common.

After all, the game's the thing.

In 1923 the *News* suggested the Walking Match from Skegness to our town should be revived. Apparently a successful Walk had been held twenty years before. But this fact, as remote to we 9-year-old members of Miss Credland's Standard 3 as the Crimean war, held no interest. What did matter was the prospect of a sporting spectacle right on our doorsteps that had an added piquancy of sheer novelty.

Appetites were whetted by tit-bits in successive issues of the *News*: a mounting interest — a committee formed — a date fixed — arrangements nearing completion — many entrants. More tangibly we could sometimes see the said entrants training, manfully striding out accompanied by a cloth-capped cyclist rather enjoying his conspicuous supporting role. These training sessions disproved any notion of a walking race as a simple affair. A trainee might decide to 'sprint' past us showing his paces to small fry, arms swinging mightily so that at the highest point tips of extended fingers were almost level with his nose. Once past, with a dwindling view of thrusting buttocks going in-out over threshing legs, one of our number was bound to say "'E's dog-'utchin'." And another to reply "'E i'nt." Thus starting an argument. Dog-'utchin' was the inelegant term used locally when that fine dividing line between legal fast walking and illegal trotting had been broken.

The final build-up to the great day started the previous Friday with the *News* publishing the lengthy list of entrants. Although we knew many of them, at least by sight and/or reputation, spotting the winner was difficult if not impossible. Len Cox guarded Athletic's goal efficiently but could he walk the 21 miles — in part a Wolds switchback — in under four hours? In experience George Kidd, the 1903 winner, surpassed everybody, but surely even a fit middle-aged man couldn't triumph again. The towering, slim Roy Coney, scion of our leading gents' outfitting firm, had very long legs, but did that willowy frame carry sufficient stamina? And so on.

The race was fixed for a Wednesday. From the Monday before playground talk concerned this one topic. Boys imitated seriously or in pardody a racing walker's style: swinging arms, wiggling posterior, legs going like pistons and all. Contestants' chances were debated ad nauseam. Wednesday morning found us in a fever similar to when Town and Athletic clashed in a cup-tie. That afternoon Miss Credland's words on parsing in general and predicates in particular seemed quite irrelevant to real life. But at playtime we knew, barring acts of God, a local dignitary had lowered a flag at Roman Bank, Skegness and started the walkers on their journey.

On the way home from school shreds of news that had come through by telephone were passed on by grown-ups. They, too, were infected by this time and agog as any child. They said the race had started at the scheduled 3 o'clock, that the pack was no longer a pack before Skegness was left behind, and the walkers were really strung out by the time the leaders reached Burgh-le-Marsh, roughly quarter of the distance.

Two days later the *News* reported "... High Toynton Road was thronged with people at the time of the finish. Perhaps never before has there been such a dense crowd in East Street or in the Bull Ring and the Market Place." Very true. Nor did Walk crowds in succeeding years (the event just had to be repeated!) ever seem to equal that multitude of a June evening in 1923. I had not realised our town and its environs possessed so many souls (nor, it may be assumed, did a lot of adults). Literally everyone appeared to be abroad, infant and ancient, from robustly fit to the halt and lame. Mother and I took up position near the Market Place finishing post soon after 6 o'clock. As we walked a crush of people moved in both directions intent on either meeting the first walkers home or, like us, seeing them finish.

An old photograph showing our section of the Market Place crowd provides a reminder of near-forgotten details. That the crowd, six or eight deep, spilled on to the roadway; that the old Post Office had a round clock inserted high in its window; that several youths obtained a grandstand view by standing on the Midland Bank's railings; that the evening must have been unseasonably chill judging from spectators' coats and scarves. And the photograph illustrates excellently what folk of both sexes and all ages were wearing in 1923.

That night, of course, no one bothered his or her head about fashions. All talk concerned the walkers; how a fancied contestant had dropped out halfway home, how both women competitors at last intelligence were going well, that a leading half dozen were bunched at Slash Hollow — the bush telegraph worked overtime. Then an exciting item passed through the crowd like wildfire: Sid Stones had shaken off all rivals and was over Dunham's Hill. Therefore he must now be only about a mile away, a mile all downhill. You could feel the crowd's tension increase as the minutes ticked by.

Then, in addition to the buzz of talk and shuffling feet, a new sound could be heard. Like rustling leaves and barely discernible at first, it grew louder and louder we realised it was a combination of cheering and clapping. The sound swelled until, as Sid Stones rounded Sharp's corner and entered our range of vision, we were enveloped in a solid wall of sound. Not only was he followed by the cyclist who had accompanied him all the way but also by a score of excited boys as if he was some latter day Piped Piper. Sweat plastered Sid's hair to his forehead and darkened his red collarless jersey, his boots were heavily dust coated. But he walked well and looked in good fettle as he breasted the finishing tape, broadly smiling and a little bemused by the tumult.

Sid Stones had beaten George Kidd's 1903 time by five minutes. Six minutes later the second man arrived, a bare half-minute before Len Cox, and the first ten came within a space of 21 minutes. The 1903 winner came in fifth to receive an ovation nearly as big as Sid Stones'. So did the two ladies, well down the field but many had doubted their capacity to finish. Competitors clocked in every few minutes. They wore football jerseys, plain and striped, over or tucked into baggy shorts that were white, black or any conceivable shade of blue. Some wore caps, a few, including the lofty Roy Coney, proper athletes' vests. Two characters came in with arms around each other's neck (whether for mutual assistance or friendship or both was not clear) and were bracketed in umpteenth place. The two ladies walked in demurely, wearing plain and quite long dresses (short skirts were three or four years away).

A marvellous evening that was mulled over for weeks and weeks. It was clear that the famous London to Brighton Walk could never have given greater pleasure and excitement.

"A'yer goin' t'the Gaily?"

You would probably be asked the question many times around the end of July during those blissful first days of the 6-week summer holiday. Days when the prospect of renewing struggles with vulgar fractions and teacher tantrums seemed remote as winter snow. The word 'Gaily' stood for Gala. Your average inhabitant would no more have pronounced it 'ghala' as pronounce grass 'grahss'. 'Gaily' was a good exmaple of local usage: a four-letter word of two syllables with both mutilated.

The annual Gala on August Bank Holiday always drew a big crowd to the Oaks Meadow — a changed Oaks Meadow to that of a soccer season. Marquees dotted its outskirts; the pitch, now innocent of goal-posts, with running- and cycle-track markings replacing touch-lines and the rest; and ice-cream stalls and refreshment tents enjoying excellent business. A different type of crowd attended too. Not the almost wholly male football throng but one of whole families making the most of the last general holiday before Christmas.

They found much to entertain them on a warm summer afternoon surrounded by sufficient fellow townsmen to satisfy the most gregarious. Athletes came from far and wide, for this was one of Lincolnshire's chief meetings and certain county championships were decided. Starters' pistols cracked, white vested sprinters sped in their glamorous spiked shoes, distance runners loped round the big circle conserving energies for final bursts. It was all very fascinating, not least because of having a rare opportunity of seeing correctly clad athletes, thus aiding imaginations when reading the stories in boys' periodicals. But we could not be partisan in these Gala events for no local competed.

There was, however, a local cyclist to be cheered on, although I think we would have preferred the cycling anyway. It engendered great excitement: stripped down bikes, riders crouched over low handlebars with faces contorted and legs flailing on the pedals. Narrow tyred wheels constantly fighting for the circular track's white line, apparently drawn like iron filings to a magnet. Round and round they raced, mops of hair and vests of many colours ruffled by the breeze, sometimes standing on their pedals to get more leverage.

Occasionally when jockeying for position wheels would touch causing an almighty pile-up, but fortunately it was only occasional. Competing wheels usually missed each other by the narrowest of margins and I trembled for the riders in a not unpleasing state compounded of ecstasy and foreboding — you just had to keep watching despite possible blood-letting. Our man, Walter Camp, all in white and composed of demeanour, rode well but, like the others, had to give best to Sammy Crickmore of Grimsby. It often happens in solo sports that an individual emerges from the ranks of the merely good into a class of his own. Such an exemplar was the smiling Sammy for more than one Gala and at other meetings too. Machine and rider merged into one as he streaked past rivals in race after race no matter what the handicapping, his prominence emphasised by a black and yellow hooped vest. Wasp colours did indeed seem fitting.

Small boys could really identify with competitors when the inter-school events were held — perhaps they were the most popular of the Gala's programme. To our shrill excitement our own Wesleyan School team made a clean sweep in 1922, and this after winning the cup the previous year. What heroes they were, running and jumping as if inspired, the crowd cheering as loudly as for any adult event.

And the sun shone down genially as it manifestly should have done.

SEVEN : THIS LITTLE PIGGIE WENT TO MARKET

No doubt about it, waking up on a Saturday morning *was* different. Before full consciousness a kind of semi-aware anticipation, of knowing the day ahead took in most of the weekly outside pleasures. A day when the enticing pull of my feather bed could be safely indulged a little longer. Yet not for too long; Saturday time was too valuable for squandering on wakeful lay-ins.

By 1923 and attendance at the afternoon children's matinée a weekly high spot, morning happenings occurred as regularly as the local paper's appearance the previous day. A succession of callers at half-hourly intervals —paper girl, milkman, baker (all requiring payment) and butcher boy in that order, and possibly the postman. Our paper girl rejoiced in the name of Amelia, which I found hilariously funny and made a point of telling her so every Saturday. Poor Amelia.

About eleven o'clock the black bulk of the Hagworthingham carrier's cart lumbered past, the carrier himself darkly clothed and inscrutable as a sphinx. Partly glimpsed occupants seemed like waxworks, quite quiet and staring out of the dusky interior, less animated even than the carrier. Only a slight creaking, plodding hooves and the big wheels grating on flint-faced road could be heard.

The cart's coming was a chief confirmation that another market day had arrived.

In earliest recollection market day is entangled with visits to our butcher's. Before schooldays and for a little while afterwards, Grandma and I went there each Saturday afternoon. For Grandma it was a call that combined business and pleasure, Mrs. Hurst, the butcher's wife, being a friend. Or, if not exactly a friend, an admirable partner in detailed discussions of current topics.

The shop was a typical butcher's establishment. Wicked looking hooks impaled the ceiling at irregular intervals, a small wood and glass office occupied one corner and the floor had brown tiles. On our entry Mrs. Hurst emerged from her office and always sat me on a little stool which, she said, was specially reserved for this purpose. Not true, of course, and intended to convey that, on being seated comfortably, I should be seen and not heard. The ladies talk seemed interminable. The cost of living, weddings, deaths, illnesses, the best jobbing builder to employ, the fight to get a gaslamp near our house, what relations were doing, what reply an annoying rate-collector received — subject matter was endless. If another customer entered, he or she would be served and speedily despatched with conversation resumed at the precise point of interruption. The butcher, traditional blue and white striped apron taut over a portly midriff, took little part in the talk, just adding a monosyllable here and there. Finally, at long last, Grandma intimated whether beef or mutton would be her pleasure, expertly chose a cut, and paid for this and the other meat (a standing order for

Saturday's special high tea) which the errand boy had delivered that morning.

Grandma apparently thought that her enjoyable conversation with Mrs. Hurst satisfactorily concluded, I had earned a treat. In summer, this could be a visit to the ice cream stall. Or, if a fair was in town, a ride on the roundabouts. Or, best of all, we sometimes went to the cinema: the afternoon matinée, sitting well back from the front rows of seething juveniles that, some time ahead, would be my territory too. But some of the films seen with Grandma were frightening, two haunting my dreams long afterwards. A newsreel showing a deceased Roman Catholic dignitary lying in state (it is uncertain which haunted more, the waxen face or the strange ornate vestments). And a film showing a building which had collapsed on a Mexican bandit. Above the piled bricks appeared one of his hands grasping despairingly at the air and then relapsing gradually into absolute stillness.

All through the 'Twenties one felt the onset of market day on Fridays. In the afternoons you entered our Kitchen to be greeted by the scent of liberally applied floor polish and to find the table top scrubbed a positively snowy white. Judging from a teasing lingering odour of pastry, the scrubbing had followed Grandma's weekly baking.

Friday evening was enlivened by Mother bringing in the *News*. Grandma claimed first look and treated us to advance information of outstanding tit-bits. Garnished naturally with apposite comment — satisfaction that Henry Edwards or Matheson Lang were appearing in the coming week's films, a cluck of disapproval at a police court case, surprise that so-and-so was not among the listed mourners at a funeral.

In the meantime Grandad struggled with his piece-work book. This was a penny notebook in which he entered jobs done during the week and handed in to his works office first thing Saturday morning. This was an important operation as wages were involved. He sat with furrowed brow wearing Grandma's reserve spectacles (he never did get a personal pair), writing with the stub of pencil that he always preferred to a full length one.

We all knew Grandad must not be disturbed during these calculations. They bothered him far more than any manual task. And bothered him increasingly as time went on — a state of affairs made worse by an unspoken conviction no one could help. However, during the 1930s, nearing 80 and working a few hours a week at the pleasure of his firm's proprietor, he did sometimes enlist my aid. But my (to him) too rapid calculations proved unnerving to Grandad and he would spend the rest of the evening going over them again and again.

On Friday evenings planks and stall ends gave advance notice of the morrow's market, propped against trees bordering the Market Place. Trees, incidentally, which a few years later had their branches ruthlessly pruned in supposed pollarded style, but in the 'Twenties stretching a full span. In full leaf they were seven gently swaying sentinels with trunks guarded from initial-scratching penknives by tall corsets of chestnut stakes. It was the last Friday duty of Council workmen to lug stall components from a nearby store ready for assembly early next morning. This did not take long. The two ends positioned, a few planks thrust across the middle spars, a tarpaulin roof spread over the end tops and there you were.

One Market Place stall, though, was not in the workmen's province. This was a little wood hut trundled gratingly on its iron wheels to a time honoured spot. A flap pushed up at the front provided an awning for customers and created a serving window for the vendors. They sold icecream, mainly to a juvenile clientele in the form of penny cornets. An old married couple, Mr. and Mrs. Danby, ran the stall and were the market's greatest institutions, as indispensible to the Saturday scene as the cinema's tuppenny matinée.

Three stalls hugged the bend into High Street's eastern end, a broad meeting point of four streets. More stalls skirted this section outside the Bull and Red Lion. One or two were occupied by shopkeepers who had stationed them in front of their shops, but in the main stall holders were one-day vendors. A fairly regular Market Place visitor, selling cut-price crockery, had a nice line in hectoring banter. Greasy looking and reminiscent of the traditional racing tout, he harangued a constantly changing circle drawn as if to a raree-show. Most locals surveyed him stolidly, on their guard and determined not to be taken in. Yet his goods looked reasonable value for the prices asked and his flamboyance welcome to market day loiterers.

Saturdays might have been joy days for school children, a respite to their teachers and brought a noon-time finish to certain toilers. But for most of the employed, however, the day signified the week's hardest. Grocers and clothiers kept open until eight o'clock while those shutting at an everyday six were much busier than on other days. It was the most exacting day, too, for bank clerks and office workers, their sevices in demand from the district's farming community whose Saturday custom it was to descend on the town. A community that, even in those 'Twenties days of depressed agriculture, formed the town's main support. Farmers sustained the agricultural implement firms, did much to keep the two saddlers in business, were responsible (one suspects) for the presence of three national bank branches and definitely responsible for auctioneers' thriving farming accounts sections. Their ranks provided several J.P's and Grammar School governors, members of elementary school management committees, pillars of our Wesleyan chapel and, of course, they monopolised the Rural District Council. A ruddy complexioned, often gaitered and tweed hatted band, shrewd and professional as any group in Lincolnshire.

The young employees cycled to town in the early evening to sample urban delights of cinema and pub. As a child lying half awake in bed, I sometimes heard them returning, their loud guffaws and broad vowelled raillery loosened by a few pints of beer. The young labourers' lot was a hard one so nobody minded this mild weekend carousal.

The solicitors' offices, an adjoining twain made sombre by a dark alley situation, owed some Saturday activity to the police court held that morning, proceedings that received full treatment in the following Friday's *News*. The cases were for the most part of a minor nature — a man cycling without a lamp after dark, a trivial motoring offence and the like. But there could be a maintenance order against a young man for getting a girl 'in trouble' to titillate the readership. "The lass allust brings 'er trouble 'oo-am", people said time and again in a parrot-like litany.

Saturday nights in the town ...

By six o'clock the tempo would change. All Market Place stalls had packed up some time before. An increasingly hoarse crockery vendor was first to go —to an unimaginable destination (unkind townsmen reckoned he kept his money under a mattress like certain locals were reputed to do). But one High Street stall, a fruiterer's, continued in business, lit in dark months by a sputtering naphtha jet. A different and, in the main, younger throng occupied the streets. Purposeful shoppers had been replaced by relaxed folk who tended to stand talking on pavement edges.

At seven o'clock on dark Saturdays the Market Place presented the greatest contrast to earlier hours. On one side two unrelieved stretches of blackness —closed banks — accentuated the brightness of shops there. Similarly on the Post Office side with a couple of shops at one end. These belonged to a newsagent, enjoying a healthy trade in football editions, and a fried fish shop, limbering up for the week's best patronised session.

Mid-evening and the local Salvation Army band moved into position near the memorial. Bonneted Salvation Army lassies fanned out among spectators clutching copies of *War Cry* which would mostly be sold in town centre pubs a little later. By the time of the band's departure shop assistants were thankfully hoisting shutters. The cinema, pubs and clubs had creamed off almost all pedestrians.

Soon after ten o'clock and High Street became animated again as the cinema disgorged its audience, the pubs their patrons and the clubs their members. An hour later and only the fish shops were open. The last customers and two patrolling policemen had the town centre all to themselves.

Each Saturday morning a couple of pennies appeared on the Kitchen mantelpiece. They were always in the same place: near to the right-hand end and a polished wood ornament that resembled an outsize chess piece. To a child, adults' ways are often, for good or ill, predictable; on this occasion the pennies represented the nicest manifestation of routine. For they were the 'open sesame' to the afternoon's film matinée, in pre-teen years an ordinary week's unchallenged high spot.

It was also a matter of routine that Grandma cooked an 'easy' Saturday dinner (she afterwards cooked a high tea as well). Easy or no, the meal was delicious: traditional Lincolnshire sausages of high meat content fried to a delightful crispness, succulent as any ripe fruit. Thus fortified and just tidy enough to pass inspection, I was ready for the road.

Before reaching the Town bridge you noticed many intimations of market day. More people were abroad. Errand boys, transformed for the day from mere schoolboys to wage earners, cycled importantly by. Some wore aprons, confirming working status. Shadowy outlines of men's backs could be discerned on Plough, Cross Keys and Greyhound windows where, on ordinary days, only chair and settle backs were visible.

At the Town bridge the market really revealed itself. Outside an auctioneer's, long compartmentised cages on trestles contained chickens and geese clucking away clamorously. Whether the birds objected or approved of public exhibition was unclear. A little farther on, stalls lined the pavement right round the 90-degree bend into High Street. At this corner a leathery aroma from a saddler's open door mixed incongruously with that from piled produce on a fruiterer's stall. It was a sign you were almost there.

Squat and grey, the cinema straddled High Street's middle ground. It had been built some seventy years before as a corn exchange and still housed a corn merchant's office at the front. By this time a steady stream of juveniles would be making for the little box office where the proprietor's wife took our tuppences. The proprietor himself frequently stood nearby. When clad in breeches, as he often was, he put one in mind — doubtless thanks to occasional perusals of *Boys' Cinema* — of a contemporary film director. Only the back-to-front peaked cap and megaphone were missing.

The cinema had a high ceiling spanned at intervals by hammer beams, and possessed a dimness, even with lights fully on, that was compounded by its dark blue walls and black painted dado. The front eight or so rows contained us tuppenny patrons, the rest of the hall being but thinly populated at matinées. Our rows quickly filled with a chattering, munching, sucking, sprawling, laughing, squealing, sometimes clandestinely smoking, mob. Biggest juveniles occupied the forms further from the screen and one gravitated there over the years by seniority (as at school, big 'uns ruled the roost). As a little 'un in the front rows, your head when gazing at the sceen seemed to assume the tilt necessary for looking at a near-overhead aeroplane.

Before a performance began, should noise and events get too extreme — say boys amiably wrestling on the dusty floor or, less amiably, actually fighting —Ed, an attendant, intervened. An interesting character this Ed. Of unguessable age, rumour had it he was quite hairless and certainly no one of our acquaintance had even seen him capless. Beyond any conjecture, though, was an astonishing loquacity to bear on any and every subject. Not necessarily uninformed talk either. A decade later his early reminiscences of early cinema in bioscope days I found fascinating. But in those tuppenny matinées one saw Ed only as a restorer of comparative peace, his steady drone directed at wrongdoers like a verbal hosepipe. His attire never changed: cap, tweed jacket with bulging pockets, grey flannel trousers and brown boots.

Through all the tremendous din girls kept a studious unawareness of masculine high spirits, talking primly among themselves and keeping a wary eye on any tagging-along infants. Peace came magically when the lights dimmed, everybody immediately absorbed with the screen. The pianist for evening performances did not play at matinées. Instead a panatrope — an electric contrivance that played gramophone records through a loudspeaker —blared forth. Before long these records were as familiar as the old traditional songs learned at school. Almost certainly no one in those turbulent tuppenny rows could have put a name to any of them, however. Now it can be said that whoever selected the records nourished a leaning towards nineteenth century operatic overtures. For staple fare included the overtures to "Zampa",

Harold Lloyd .

Tom Mix .

William Farnum.

Wallace Reid.

"Raymond", "William Tell", "Masaniello" and "Maritana". Stirring screen action was a signal for the playing of Balfe's overture to "The Bohemian Girl" or Suppé's "Morning, Noon and Evening in Vienna". Whenever I chance to hear any of them now, recollection of those Saturday afternoons returns. The initial hubbub and instant silence as the films started; the growing underfoot litter of toffee papers, peanut shells and orange peel; young faces lifted screenwards in sure knowledge of being richly entertained. The one occasion when Wesleyan Swilltubs and Church Humbugs intermingled in harmony. And indeed when M, then a Church Humbug, and I first met to discover a kindred taste in many things. The first of these — a liking for dates which had a value beyond the consumption thereof. The stones were handy for flicking at the napes of girls' necks.

Felix the film cat.

Boys in the tuppenny seats were decided in likes and dislikes. Strong action films had us galvanised. A hero with an unsuspecting back turned and a villain creeping up behind would cause many a shout of "Look out!" We gave vent to quite involuntary cheers as a hero-led posse charged to a rescue. Even increasing discernment that enabled one to notice horses galloped repeatedly round the same mountain did not reduce enjoyment. No doubt Western stars' glamour helped here. Tom Mix, William and Dustin Farnum and grim faced Buck Jones had but to appear on the screen and perceived imperfections were as naught. Similarly with Elmo Lincoln as Tarzan or Wallace Reid. And most of all with the elder Douglas Fairbanks, whose athletic feats had every boy in the hall on his seat edge.

As popular — perhaps more so — were the two-reel comedies with Charlie Chase, Harry Langdon, Snub Pollard, Andy Clyde, Chester Conklin, Ben Turpin, Louise Fazenda, Lupino Lane et el. Glorious custard pie throwing,

87

"The grocery store where Mother worked ...".

banana skin slipping, fire escape falling, slapstick stuff. Films where trick camera work gave us hair-raising car chases with hair-breadth misses at crossroads, traffic cops jumping for dear life, and races with out-of-control locomotives. Sometimes — what joy! — *two* comedies were shown. And if the main picture was a comedy then life held no greater rapture. Harold Lloyd's "Safety Last", for example, in which he climbed a skyscraper undergoing vertigo-inducing adventures all the way, and we laughed and palpitated in turn.

As exciting as car chases was the serial, which lasted three months in weekly instalments. Where each episode (except the last) left the hero and/or heroine in so dire a situation escape seemed unimaginable. Where heroines were tied to railway lines with a train due any minute, and heroes hung by tips of fingers over precipices (thus bringing about the term 'cliff-hanger'). Charles Hutchinson ("Hurricane Hutch") and Ruth Roland often appeared in serials as hero and heroine. She faced almost as many dangers as did Hurricane Hutch. So nobody repined when they came together in the final episode, presumably to live happily ever after. To we boys this happy ending differed from love scenes in big romantic films. Rudolph Valentino's torrid encounters with painted lipped vamps elicited our feigned boredom, whistles and groans (though no doubt girls were goggle-eyed). We unkindly dubbed him Rudolph Vaselino and his film "Four Horsemen of the Apocalypse" we renamed "Four Horsemen of the Eucalyptus". His films had plenty of action, however. "Blood and Sand" (disgracefully referred to locally as "Blood and Snot") served as introduction to the Spanish bull ring, jumping back in mind like a half-remembered song when Ernest Hemingway entered my reading life in the 'Thirties.

After two blissful hours the lights went up. We trooped out, momentarily blinking in strong daylight and slowly coming back to earth. But, from September to April, the afternoon's entertainment was not necessarily over: the Town F.C. might have a home fixture. So we ran all the way to the Wong. The match would be in its second half, the gate unattended and we could get in free.

Wasn't life wonderful?

The grocery store where Mother worked kept open until eight o'clock on Saturdays and, due to cashing up and straightening up, she seldom returned before ten. She took a snatched lunch in the shop's rear room, returning briefly for Saturday's high tea.

After tea one pre-wireless autumn evening and Mother regretfully departed until after my bedtime, Grandma said "Would you like to play cards?"

Life constantly presents new experiences for small children. I nodded vigorously.

"Grandad'll play too," Grandma added, "won't you, Dadder?" (Very occasionally she addressed him as Dadder, his pet name when my uncles and aunts were children).

"Aye," replied Grandad. And I sensed my grandparents felt, it being Saturday night, a special activity was called for.

Thus did card playing Saturdays start. The fire banked up, the Kitchen table covered with a thick olive green cloth, Grandma at one corner near the fire,

Grandad at the other and me having the far side all to myself. Grandma with a battered cribbage board on which were impaled three match sticks to chart our progress no matter what game was being played. She could expertly shuffle a pack of cards in an impressively unconcerned manner. Grandad and I never approached this facility. Nor could we hold a hand of cards so well: a neat, near-closed fan that showed every card's suit and value in the smallest possible compass. In extenuation, my fingers were small and inexperienced while Grandad's, broad and work-hardened, had adapted to rougher demands in handling large leather hides.

The introduction to playing cards followed initiations given by Grandma into other indoor pastimes. We had started with Ludo, a game of chance, and graduated to Halma, a game demanding skill. Nobody ever beat Grandma at Halma. She ruled the board's 256 squares like a queen, her pieces leaping over opponents' pieces in a series of scintillating and ingeniously plotted moves. She gracefully descended to my level again in simple affairs like Snap and Happy Families, which were in fact card games but not in the sense that Grandma meant when enquiring on that autumn evening whether I would like to play cards.

"We'll play Beggar my Neighbour," Grandma had then continued, "it'll teach you the value of the cards."

It did. The simplist of games, each player received the same number of cards face down, did not look at them and then played them in sequence one at a time. Each round played, the highest card took the trick, suits having differing values.

'Y'deal me some owry 'ands," Grandad would say to Grandma in shock reproof. As if for consolation he might light a Manikin whiff, an act reserved for weekends and holiday times, and the Kitchen acquired the blue cigar haze that went so well with relaxed occasions.

Card values learned, we later turned to Grandma's favourite Whist. Three-handed Whist was fun. The dummy hand might hold valuable trumps, a fact unclear until the end of a game unless someone boldly led trumps. Another favourite game of Grandma's was Black Lady, in which the Queen of Spades was the key card. The detailed rules have faded from memory, but cards were passed from one player to the next and the chief aim was not to be left with the Black Lady at the game's conclusion.

I rather suspect Grandad preferred Dominoes (which we also played on Saturdays) to card games. Perhaps he played at the Cross Keys for small stakes. At all events he held his dominoes in the easy manner one sees with seasoned pub practitioners — arm laid along the table, hand arched round dominoes in a protective crescent — while I, able to hold three at most, was reduced to placing them before me like randomly spaced anti-tank blocks.

Whatever the games played, it seemed in no time at all before the grandmother clock on the wall chimed nine and for Grandma to pronounce "Last game". And it would be, cards and dominoes carefully gathered, boxed and put away. But the delightful ritual would be re-enacted next Saturday and the Saturday after that ...

Scene: the Wong. Time: any Saturday afternoon around 1928 when the Town

F.C. are at home. The team although still useful, is no longer the all-conquering one of fond memory, The leavening of old and future professionals has gone, its composition now wholly local. And naturally M and I have changed too. We have outgrown tuppenny matinées and, sad to say, developed at 14 a tincture of disrespect for matters hitherto treated, if not as sacrosanct, rather seriously. Crowds do not now touch one and a half thousand, having descended to a half or third of that number, but are still respectable for a small place. The thinning of crowds has served to focus attention on two gentlemen in particular, whose loud comments are regular accompaniments to every match.

They are a highly contrasting pair, standing on opposite touch-lines. One is flanked by cronies and forever laughing, the other solitary and grim. The first is a shopkeeoper who has left his wife and daughter in charge for a couple of hours. He is a short, ginger moustachioed man in an old grey suit. He stands, hands deep in trouser pockets, a fully expanded grin wreathing a jolly face. His voice is not deep but has a cutting quality transcending all noise but that made by the gentleman of the opposite touch-line. He finishes each sally with a chortle.

An opposing full-back slices a clearance and the ball skids into touch.

"Keep it on the island! Ho, ho!", cries the shopkeeper, rocking back on his heels. His cronies, pleased with this wit, take up the chant.

"Keep it on the island!"

A throw-in and again our shopkeeper's voice cuts through surrounding murmur.

"Come on Bumbler! Ho, ho!"

And Bumbler, a dark young man who is Town's right-half and runs in a remarkably high-kneed gait, tears at an opponent as if at the shopkeeper's bidding.

"He runs like a frisky horse. Ho, ho!", confides shopkeeper to his friends in a monstrous stage whisper. They agree heartily and laugh in extravagant fashion.

"Yes. Just like a frisky hoss," says one of them and volunteers an uncharacteristic addition — "Owd Tommy Bricker 'ad a cob afore th'War that galloped just like Bumbler."

"Come on Bumbler!", echo shopkeeper's cronies, still grinning at the frisky horse quip and memories of Tommy Bricker's cob.

And in such manner the group enjoy their afternoon. Moderate though the shopkeeper's wit is, it is at least good humoured, a quality that cannot be claimed by the gentleman opposite.

This is Digger. He is a labourer, his nickname stemming from the fact that his main working implements are pick, spade and shovel, all of which he can wield mightily if in the mood. You can see why. A powerful physique is obvious in his stance: thrust out barrel chest, clenched fists deep in corduroy trousers' fronting horizontal pockets, taut arms and legs certainly well muscled.

But on this occasion burliness is not Digger's main characteristic. Now it is the combination of beetling brow and baleful glare. And, of course, the voice.

The voice comes out as a bellow, deep from the recesses of his being, ominous as a thunder clap.

"Are yer blind, ref?"

You feel menace behind the words. There is not a vestige of the shopkeeper's good humour: Digger's contributions are sheer malice. M and I, separated by the width of the pitch from Digger, joke about him. I make the customary sally lifted from Frank Richards's Greyfriars stories about the Bull of Bashan's roar, but we sense also the hardness of the man.

"Weers yer bluddy specs, ref?" he bellows, confirming my Bull of Bashan comparison.

In spite of the evident displeasure and scowl and creased brow, I suppose that in a warped way Digger is enjoying himself. After a hard week he is letting off steam against his lot, his risen ire fuelled by the intake of mid-day pints.

Our two foghorns are not the only distractions from activity on the field of play. We stand near the centre line, ten yards or so from shopkeeper and company. With us is an adult acquaintance of M's, possessor of an enormous grin and the nickname Wo (which I take to be short for Walter). It transpires Wo is a friend of a Town winger who thus half lurks on our touch-line. (These, remember, are the days when players' duties are pretty strictly defined: full-backs defend, half-backs operate between backs and forwards, forwards concentrate on attacking. And wing forwards keep to their touch-lines, cutting in only rarely). This winger takes his function literally. When play is in the region of Town's goal he comes to chat with Wo.

"Dirty divil that back, kid," says Wo, who addresses both minors and grown men thus.

"He bluddy is," replies our winger, who answers to the name of Matt, "but I'll sort 'im aht".

Matt is a dark, gangling man, tall for a winger. What you most notice are his large feet set splay whether he is walking, running or stationary.

The enemy attack is repulsed and the ball heftily cleared in Matt's direction. He says hastily "See yer in a minnit, Wo," and clumps upfield like an ungainly nag. The dirty full-back also goes for the ball and he and Matt tangle untidily, the ball trickling into touch. Matt gets up holding a knee but the full-back lies writhing on the ground. The visiting trainer runs on to find the legendary magic sponge is out of magic on this occasion and the full-back is carried off.

A throw-in is taken and play meanders to the far side. Matt returns to our little group.

"Don't think 'e'll gi' us any more trouble," says Matt laconically, "I rammed my knee in 'is guts blind side o' the ref."

The ball comes in Matt's direction again. Before clumping off he says "It were an accident, o' course. I said 'Sorry'." And he gave Wo a conspiratorial wink.

EIGHT : ALWAYS ON SUNDAY

As on Saturdays, Sunday awakenings in the early 'Twenties had a distinctive feel. Not this time, however, a quickening anticipation; rather a luxurious languor born of realising Monday-to-Friday's iron timetable did not on this day exert its tyranny. Even Grandad, that most inveterate of early weekday risers, lay a decent while. One hovered untroubled, therefore, in the delicious borderland betwixt sleep and full consciousness.

On light summer mornings resident sparrows and starlings and Mr. Blades's chickens seem reverentially muted. Rarely did a human voice penetrate our dozes although humanly induced sounds might. The local Salvation Army band played in West Street one week and our road the next, its volume unimpaired by Saturday night stints in the Market Place. Not near our house fortunately, but nearly quarter of a mile away. Their music nonetheless could carry on the quiet air, cornets and trombones slightly unsure, euphoniums growling in a lower register, bass drum being heartily whacked. The scene could easily be imagined. A blue uniformed circle round the Captain, taking up most of the road's width, undisturbed by traffic limited to an occasional bicycle. Between band numbers a prayer and an address from the Captain, bonneted Army lassies standing with tambourines clasped behind their backs, heartfelt "Hallelujah" interjections coming from the men.

A couple of hours later, around 10.0 a.m. nothing at all interrupted the town's tranquillity. Tempo was at its lowest as if extra liveliness at yesterday's market had sapped all energies. No gossiping groups adorned the Town bridge. A dog or two would wander aimlessly past shuttered shops. The few people abroad were mainly churchgoers, a shade stiff in best clothes, or patrons of a briefly opened newsagent.

Young life pulsed just as strongly as on ordinary days. But still, even in this decade of loosened habits, the fact of Sabbath observance quelled any overt expression. For the adult generations had been born in Victoria's reign and adults 'ruled the roost'. Or at any rate they did in the provincial East Midlands.

At this time there were five places of worship in the town, neatly, if fortuitously, spaced. The church stood plumb central overlooking a corner of the Market Place. Congregational and Wesleyan chapels lay east, a stone's throw apart. The west boasted a Primitive chapel and the south the Salvation Army hall. Which leaves the north: not irreligious, mark you (for several worthy Wesleyan families lived in that quarter), but devoid of churches and chapels.

In most guide-books only the church got a mention. Mediæval and by far the oldest building, its greenstone exterior had a certain charm, a quiet comeliness. And scythes on a wall within gave a regular reminder of a nearby Civil War skirmish of 1643. (Very likely a spurious reminder as any Civil War connection has never been proved). Unusually the vicarage was a fair distance away — at the end of our road. It lurked rather mysteriously among trees on rising ground, a large mid-Victorian house designed for large clerical families.

Ranking next in age — built 1821/22 — the Congregational chapel stood back from East Street; plain and square and weathered and bearing the inscription INDEPENDENT CHAPEL. Plain, too, the Primitive chapel, obliquely sited on a side street bend with its fronting road so narrow as to prevent one standing back and taking in its proportions.

The Salvation Army had taken over a church built for the Baptists who, like the Roman Catholics, had ceased to maintain a community locally. The building had adapted well to Army needs, a sizeable congregation-facing platform comfortably taking bandsmen and instruments. The wall behind them carried a brightly painted scroll on which were the words BLOOD AND FIRE.

Only rarely did I see these interiors and might not have seen them at all but for a temporarily domiciled aunt who sampled places of worship as connoisseurs sample wine vintages. Their appendage buildings were entered on secular occasions, i.e. the Church House (the old Grammar School which had become a parish hall) for magic lantern shows and the Congregational Sunday School for concerts. One of these was long remembered for a performer's spirited rendering of "Ukelele Lady", accompanying himself with a ukelele. Around this time (1925) ukes were very much an 'in' instrument and, by general consent, his rendition was regarded as extremely sophisticated.

In contrast to seldom visited venues, 'our' Chapel and Sunday school were, of course, as familiar as Miss Stothard's sweet shop. As such they must receive lengthier treatment.

Seating a thousand our Chapel, by small town standards, must have been in the monster class. It dated from 1870 and was naturally the most imposing of two formidable Wesleyan buildings in Queen Street. The Chapel building also contained, at its rear, the Band Room, so named from such rooms' original purpose for bands of Wesleyans meeting there and not because of the Boys' Brigade instruments lodged there. This had, too, a more active role as meeting room for Chapel organisations such as the Wesley Guild.

Besides being imposing the Chapel was also an architectural hybrid. Frontally the two ends, set forward from a centre section incorporating Georgian entrance doors, were topped by classical pediments. And the many uniform windows punctuating all four sides on both storeys were Baroque. Inside the feel of sheer size predominated. The ground floor formed the well of a circular gallery from most of which polished wood pews rose steeply almost to ceiling level in the manner of an amphitheatre. The remainder of the gallery was taken up by the organ whose pipes reached ceilingwards like a row of variously sized giant pencils embedded point down over the blind organist's stops and keyboards. Under the pipes and over the organist's loft ran an inscription in old lettering, PRAISE YE THE LORD. Fronting and parallel with the organ were two rows of choir pews, indicated by raised brass rails in front of them for holding hymn books, lady members in the front row, gentlemen behind.

The pulpit, tall on four thick legs, had been placed to face the congregation in a setting perfectly balanced symmetrically. Identical flights of steps led to it. Within a surrounding rail twin marble-topped tables had similarly arranged bowls of flowers. On the wall behind the pulpit steps were boards on which the commandments appeared, Numbers 1 to 5 on the left, 6 to 10 on the right. Finally this wall possessed, beyond the rail, identical doors, from one of which the preacher emerged.

As always, preachers came in two categories: ordained and lay, professional and amateur as it were. The first, our two resident ministers plus an occasional visitor, were, of course, instantly recognisable in dog collar and clerical grey. The lay species, known in Methodist terms as local preachers, had more variety and not only in the obvious instance of attire. They delivered sermons in every conceivable style from the informal to the earnest evangelical, although only old local preachers ranted in a fiercely declamatory, impassioned way. Conversely, only the spare gentleman from Belchford achieved so high a degree of passivity, despite a glum seriousness indolently leaning on one side of the pulpit. His mouth did not seem to open a normal width and I would silently speculate whether popping a cork between his upper and lower teeth would assist in the opening. (A prime example, this gentleman, of incorrect first impressions. Ten years on and an office colleague, he turned out to have an impish sense of humour and an encyclopædic knowledge of the great pre-1914 Sunderland soccer team). And then there was that pillar of the Chapel, occasionally taking a service instead of occupying his pew under the tablet that commemorated the Great War fallen. He held many public appointments — Urban District Councillor, Justice of the Peace, member of many committees — besides his Chapel stewardship and lay preaching. Long standing public activities had earned him deference. Accordingly his delivery in the pulpit was assured and one recalls clearly, even after sixty years, his straight-backed little figure and (by then unique) Victorian cravat.

Around 1921 the town became accustomed to seeing our junior resident minister on weekdays in mufti. He had a growing reputation as a powerful preacher, a reputation extending beyond circuit boundaries. But it appeared he had doubts concerning his vocation, hence the mufti. These doubts, however, were eventually resolved and he stayed in the ministry, shortly afterwards moving to Kent. For some years his visits as a guest preacher drew large congregations. Large congregations were now exceptional. On average Sunday mornings there would be about thirty adults, concentrated mainly in the ground pews. The numerous empty spaces, particularly in the gallery's mounting tiers, gave mute testimony to the post-war decline in religious observance.

But packed congregations could be guaranteed for certain occasions, especially for the Anniversary in early summer. Then even the high reaches of gallery pews were occupied. When the assembly rose for a hymn there was such a shuffling of feet, rustling of clothing and clearing of throats that even these unavoidable preliminaries were impressive. And if the hymn was an old favourite and rhythmical like "All things bright and beautiful", a mighty swell of voices almost drowned the accompanying organ. Three months later the Harvest Festival attracted perhaps the year's second largest attendance. (That is, unless the President of the Methodist Conference or some other celebrity preached, as did sometimes occur). The Harvest Festival enabled decoration-conscious elders to enjoy a field day in gathering and displaying fruits of the earth. Entering the Chapel that Sunday was not unlike stepping into a fruit market. As attention had to be paid to the puplpit, its decorations most caught the eye. Two items were sure to appear there every year. A large bunch of grapes, looking mouth-wateringly luscious, dangled from the lectern edge and, on the lectern itself, lay the year's biggest marrow, green striped and shiny.

Our family pew was situated in the gallery halfway up the slope at right angles to the pulpit. Due to a hereditary aversion to heights, this lofty position caused some discomfort intensified by the booming organ when standing for a hymn. Fortunately personal use of the pew was rare and limited to an occasional evening service. (Attendance at morning service and afternoon Sunday School was deemed sufficient — another indication of religion's slackening grip). In the mornings we trooped into Chapel from Sunday School and occupied the central front pews on ground level, oddly breaking Day School custom with girls seated on the right and boys on the left.

Conspicuous in our ranks were the half dozen or so children collectively known among ourselves as "the Union Kids". The Union referred to a large gaunt building erected some ninety years before and sited off adjoining Foundry Street. The children were orphans in the care of the local Board of Guardians who, in the next decade, would have been living in newly built Children's Homes on Mareham Road. Conspicuousness came not from physical difference but attire. The boys wore thick suits with high-collared jackets of grey herring bone pattern; the girls long-skirted navy serge frocks under white pinafores that had broad scalloped yokes. Both girls and boys had long knee-covering black stockings and the most enthusiastically scrubbed look of any of us. They were justifiably well liked, these orphans, and also attended the day School. Two at least, of my day, were subsequently adopted. I hope life has been good to each and every one.

There we sat, then, orphaned or otherwise, in those first rows of pews, hushed and still, hoping the sermon would not be overlong. Whether or not it was, my gaze would be drawn irresistibly to a marble plaque on the nearest side wall. It read:

His works
J O H N   R I V E T T
do follow him

What did it mean? I would wonder. Did this departed Mr. Rivett establish a water- or iron- or gas-works? Puzzling over the answer always seemed more interesting than the sermon.

Memory is uncertain which came first — attendance at Sunday or Day School. It is certain, however, these first forays into the wider world were close together. As at the Day School, infants had their own section, in this instance known as the Primary. It was run by Miss Hare with assistance from two other ladies. Miss Hare had been a missionary in India and local talk held that her thick piled up hair owed its deep red-gold hue to the tropical sun. (An unlikely story, I feel). She had come to the town to take up an appointment on the Grammar School staff. Six years on, her thin figure, slight limp and sharp features were encountered on most school days in Latin and Divinity Lessons and an exacting task mistress she then proved to be. However, this initial encounter gave no intimation of Miss Hare's sterner side. We were told biblical stories in the most simplistic terms, pipingly sang hymns appropriate to our tender years and sat in chairs that were precise miniature versions of the then common circular backed, rail sided office chair.

Again as at Day Shool, when seven years we transferred to the 'big' School. In size it made a worthy partner to the Chapel, being lofty as well as spatially large. Although often used in midweek — for example on dark Tuesday evenings for Boys' Brigade parades — it gave off its own special, though not unpleasant, closed-up smell in which varnished wood played a major part. Two lots of high-backed forms, with an aisle separating girls and boys, faced a platform. The platform received a rudimentary 'dressing' for Sunday School. From the side of a centrally positioned lectern stretched green blanket-like material tied to the platform's bordering rails. Luckily neither lectern nor stretched cloth obscured the clock on the facing wall (Sunday School ranked high in my personal list of disliked compulsory duties).

One of three Superintendents officiated. Seldom would it be one of our local butchers when, in hymn singing, his basso profundo voice was a strange element in an otherwise almost all-treble rendering. So duties were generally shared by the Day School headmaster, Mr. Waymouth, or Captain Boland. The latter, a retired Army regular, ran his Sunday afternoons like clockwork, just as he did his Boys' Brigade company. It was impossible to imagine it being any other way. His military bearing — shoulders well back, moustache and remaining hair close cropped — unmistakably spelt woe to sloppy inefficiency. His gravelly voiced addresses and Bible readings never falterd, no one fidgeted or allowed attention to wander; to have displeased that all-seeing eye was as unthinkable as breaking a Chapel window. Mr. Waymouth received an equal attention though, naturally, it was obtained in a schoolmasterly way. His afternoons, however, showed a benigner, Sunday-best side, with no winkling out of wrongdoers or ascertaining the depths of our ignorance.

On elevation to the main school, a child received a folder linen-reinforced card, the inner halves of which were headed 'Morning' and 'Afternoon'. Down the left-hand side the months of the year appeared, each opposite a line of five squares. On entering the Schoolroom prior to morning Chapel or for afternoon School, the card was produced at the door. There, behind a little table, sat a teacher armed with inked pad and stamper, who stamped a star in the appropriate date place on the proffered card. If you accumulated over the year a reasonable number of stars you received a book prize. My prize for 1924, "David Copperfield", a deliberate choice, stands on my shelves still. Its pages have a texture and quality reminiscent of 1940s wartime austerity, the printing and binding in keeping. These comments are in no wise intended as criticism. All books were welcome whether deliberate choice or 'pot luck', which meant for boys a work of a Victorian boys' writer such as R. M. Ballantyne and W. H. G. Kingston and, for girls, Louisa M. Alcott or Anna Sewell.

Whether on the theory that children thrive on settled routine or merely that Superintendents preferred it, an afternoon's ordering was predictable as fog in November. True, there obtained a nod favouring hymns seasonally fitting. We sang about Royal David's City in December, in September of ploughing and scattering good seed, in mid-year of summer suns glowing o'er land and sea. But the order of proceeding did not change. We sat class by class, front to back in ascending age, a teacher on each class extremity. There would be an opening hymn, a Bible reading, a divide into class groups for teachers to give their weekly talk, the return for an address and announcements from the Superintendent, a final hymn.

Individual class instruction broke up the afternoon nicely and involved, when in certain classes, a change of scene to one of the side rooms. These rooms smelled more closed up than the main hall. They were skirted by fixed pine seating that gave off a greater varnished wood aroma and was mixed with that from rexine bindings of recently purchased stacks of Bibles.

Teachers were mostly women. Certainly at this time no man took a girls' class although a woman could take a boys', but this may have been due to a shortage of men teachers. For a time my class had Miss Stallybrass as teacher. Earnest, nervous and apparently tremulous, it is a fair assumption she spent many hours during the week preparing her little Sunday pieces. Then to be delivered haltingly and diffidently as a poor woman might offer a dish to a rich relative. Some juvenile wag had dubbed her "Miss Cabbages" and of course the nickname stuck. Not a single sentence nor phrase of what she said can now be recalled. Yet I know her words were given with love by a spinster who loved other people's children. And if the words are not remembered, it is surely something she herself can be instantly recalled, unassuming and low voiced, seemingly asking such a little of life. A good, good woman.

Like a best suit our parlour ("The Room") justified its existence on Sundays. Grandad retired there immediately after his breakfast armed with the Sunday papers, leaving his customary armchair only for meals and demands of nature. Grandma kept him and a book company in the afternoons in her equally customary wicker chair. Mother had early made one of her few insistent rules: they must not be disturbed, so the hour between returning from Sunday School and tea was spent elsewhere. Around 5 o'clock and despatched to call my grandparents for tea, I rarely found them talking. Reading or no, they would be quite still; sometimes in the dusk with firelight dancing shadows on ceiling and walls. Yet a stillness conveying a kind of rapport, one that showed a marriage of almost golden wedding length had no need of extraneous conversation.

During the course of Sunday Grandad must have read almost every word of his *News of the World* and *Sunday Graphic*. But he never discussed their contents in my hearing — nor, very likely, out of it at home. (Nor did I ever hear him swear). This was though an innate sense of what was seemly when talking to woman and children and an ethos upright as his own stance. Both my

Our chapel outside.

Our chapel inside.

99

Social gathering in the Sunday schoolroom circa 1921.

Char-a-banc of the early 1920s.

grandparents had been born in 1856. Grandad had been to school and received instruction in reading, writing and arithmetic, the basic 'three R's'. Grandma, though, never went to school (compulsory education did not begin until after the Act of 1870) and taught herself to read and write. A chapel in her native Mansfield had unknowingly been the chief aid. By closely following the printed word in her hymn book — she already knew the verses by heart — the ability to read gradually evolved. Once acquired it quickly opened the way to writing and long before my time she could write fluent letters and post-cards (some happily still extant) whose sole failing is a little erratic punctuation. Grandma's taste in books never became catholic and she read, almost exclusively, romantic novels of strong story line. Thus Ethel M. Dell and Maud Diver, then at the height of their popularity, were her special favourites. This successful and hard won acquiring of literacy was typical of a determined character. Grandma brought a keen intelligence to bear on all domestic problems, naturally took the lead in decision making and our family was truly as matriarchal as one in the American Mid-West.

Enforced attendance at Chapel and Sunday School heightened enjoyment of Sabbath bonuses. Dinner, for instance, when Grandma's culinary skill had its finest weekly hour. To start, a Yorkshire pudding of supreme crispness over which was poured home made raspberry vinegar. Then the meat lifted sizzling from the oven, easy to slice because invariably tender, gravy deep brown and delicious, vegetables usually home grown. The gentry did not dine better. And tea saw the first sampling of Grandma's weekly baking and perhaps tins of salmon and fruit would be opened or an example of Mother's specialities —blancmanges and trifles — on offer. And well buttered bread cut a precise one-eighth of an inch as if by a machine, and strong tea —always tea! — from an ample pot adequate for four hearty drinkers.

Though an adult attendance at church and chapel might be falling and though an era of great change, old Sunday habits died hard. Or so it appeared early in the 'Twenties. Overt outdoor secular tasks were either not done or, if they were, done discreetly, even secretively. It was extremely rare to see a man digging his garden, painting a shed, working on an allotment (the allotments' gates would likely be locked anyway). It was unavoidable, and therefore excusable, for Mr. Blades to feed his chickens and the milkman to call. Yet, although unspoken, one felt an implication in the air that things had been arranged not quite properly. The sight of a gasworks employee going on shift or a farm labourer returning for his midday meal reinforced the implication. These Sabbath workers were somehow 'deprived', their working hours thought — to use a much later fashionable term — unsociable. They would have been thought a touch immoral if known to have willngly opted for Sunday work.

Being so few, these visible workers stood out from the obvious Sunday-best appearance of everyone else. There were also workers invisible to a street pedestrian (apart from meal-preparing housewives whose work, as everyone knows, is never done): publicans. But no undue noise came from their premises. Patrons slipped in and out, if not furtively, with proper circumspection. No trains ran to or from our terminus, the white gates at the station yard's entrance shut and padlocked, the station itself locked and shuttered. And children, forbidden to indulge in noisy weekday games, were told "In my young days we didn't play at all on Sundays and, if we wanted to read, it was the Bible or nothing." So we felt more or less well done by as we turned the pages of a *Playbox Annual* or those of a somewhat grubby copy of *Film Fun* which Billy Conwell had magnanimously passed on after Sunday School. (Gifts such as Billy's always counted for more than those from adults).

But these were the last years of almost unbroken Sunday quiet, of plainly heard bird song and roads little used. The cause, as with so much revolutionary change, the internal combustion engine. By the middle 1920s coast traffic, which menaced market stalls on summer Saturdays, ran with comparable intensity on summer Sundays. So the quietude did not reign until late morning when east bound traffic eased off and lasted only to tea time when the hordes returned homewards. On these mornings you were as likely to come up from the deeps of sleep to the sound of the earliest cars and motorbikes as to thrush and blackbird song. And you wondered again about an odd noise vehicles made as they motored up the gradient from the first bend. A noise quite normal until the vehicle passed our houses and reached "The Laurels", when it possessed of a vibrant hollowness. An air pocket, perhaps, or sound hitting the rear wing of "The Laurels". No matter, the phenomenon turned into a homely feature like the ivy under front bedroom windows and my feather bed's enveloping winter warmth.

As a side effect, the traffic produced more Sunday workers. Newly established wayside garages, which sprang up with a frequency emulated by urban milk bars a decade later, found their best petrol sales coincided with fine Sundays. The new garage east of "The Laurels" opened early and its dynamo thudded away long after dark. Towards town Mr. Young's single pump worked overtime.

And the recently arrived RAC scout could be seen cycling to his High Toynton kiosk, a mile distant up a steadily rising road. M, apparently on affable speaking terms with all adult males who qualified as characters, introduced me to this scout. "Don't for God's sake call him Clonk to his face," M had warned, "he'll break you in two." Actually the warning was unnecessary for one would as soon have done so as address the Grammar School head as Chunky. (The latter in a moment of unique and atypical unbending had once told my form his own schooldays' nickname). Mr. Clipsham, the RAC scout, possessed a strong personality. His freshly painted blue kiosk, strategically stationed where a secondary road to Greetham branched off the main highway, seemed a shade inadequate as a backcloth for it. He enjoyed company and we had but to inject an occasional monosyllable into conversation to keep him going. These near-monologues were worth hearing and continued unabated when he smartly saluted passing cars flaunting the RAC emblem. The salutes sometimes sidetracked Mr. Clipsham into making an interesting comment on the driver in question. ("Fancy having to salute that sod!" or "He phoned one day for help and — d'you know what? — his ruddy petrol tank was dry!"). An early instruction into how outward grown-up respectfulness can mask radically different opinion. And these opinions, pithily put, were to us wryly and engagingly funny. A returning theme was the War, stories told sardonically yet, to me anyway, impressively. Here, one knew, was a man's man.

Rightly deemed an unmitigated annoyance on market days, the now copious summer traffic made a free spectacle on Sunday evenings. Up and down our Spilsby Road the good townspeople sauntered from after teatime onwards, their first waves succeeded in due course by church and chapel leavers. They sauntered in pairs or en famille, children a few paces in front of their parents, taxing pavement capacity when returning strollers met the outgoing. (At that period only one side had a pavement). In spite of the milling traffic, strollers had a relaxed air, an evident enjoyment of seeing and being seen. There were many hat raisings and smiling greetings and remarks about what a lovely evening it was, and enquiries as to how Mary was doing at school, and wasn't it sad about old Mrs. Searby passing away only a couple of months after old Jack? Young children, chafing at enforced halts, stood on one leg while holding a parent's hand or skipped round the grown-ups and were told to hush and simmer down. And older children, above such kid's play, watched their elders, not speaking unless spoken to as custom decreed, but drinking in every word. ("But grown-ups do go on so, don't they?")

Meantime the motley cavalcade streamed by. Open char-a-bancs with bodies shaped like our enamel cooking dishes, cars and motorbikes in multiplicity of make and design. Cars with running-boards on which were clamped tool boxes and spare tins of petrol; and fold-down hoods and spare wheels attached to side or rear. Two-seaters incorporating a dickey — a seat folding into the boot —which made them four-seaters. Cars on solid tyres or the new balloon tyres (which arrived in mid-decade) and drivers often in helmets, goggles and leather coats, their ladies veiled just as the Edwardian pioneers were.

Knowledgeable spectators kept a watchful eye for the unusual. Something exotic from Europe perhaps — Bugatti or Lancia or Hispano-Suiza or Isotta-Fraschini — but mostly having to be satisfied with cheaper French Citroens and Peugeots although a fetching Fiat could sometimes be espied. Sometimes, too, a home produced aristocrat — an Alvis, a Bentley, a stately Rolls-Royce, say, rewarding an enthusiast's vigilance. The sparse number of glamour cars did not affect unduly a cavalcade's infinite variety. In 1925 Britain's 600,000 car owners had a choice of around 250 different makes. So chain-driven Trojans and three-wheeled Morgans and the products of Lea-Francis, Jowett, Swift, Riley, Wolseley, Singer, Dodge, Clyno, Arrol-Johnston and many more mingled with countless Fords, Morrises and Austins.

The last three easily outnumbered the rest. Scores of Ford Model T's, black like the original ugly but reliable 'Tin Lizzie', then, in 1927, their Model A including the refinement of a windscreen wiper and choice of four colours. A myriad of bull-nosed Morrises, Cowley and Oxford, that were oddly endearing, to be succeeded by the equally proliferating Morris Minor in 1928. Swarms of Austin Sevens, tiny and open and accommodating two adults, replaced (also in 1928) by the famous Baby Austin, a saloon with greater capacity. And not so numerous though still plentiful, the Vauxhall 30/98, forty years on to become synonymous with the 1920s because often used in period television dramas.

Motor-cycles ran alongside and weaved in between three- and four-wheeled

105

vehicles in a like profusion of makes. They, too, had some overwhelmingly represented: Triumph, New Hudson, Douglas, Royal Enfield, Levis, B.S.A. and a fair sprinkling of the more expensive A.J.S. and Harley-Davidson could be seen as well as the models of Scott, Matchless, Sun, James, Indian and so on. It was a point of importance that boys should know A.J.S. stood for A. J. Stevens and B.S.A. for Birmingham Small Arms (and also the latter's splendidly bawdy, if incorrect, other meaning). Sidecars, metal and wicker, were common as pillions; rider's caps, worn peak to back, common as leather helmets.

Over half a century later it is hard to realise the legal speed limit throughout the 'Twenties was only 20 miles per hour. The more so when cars like the 1925 Lancia Lambia could reach 70 mph and even modest Austin Sevens and Ford Model T's 38 and 45 mph respectively. It is said everyone exceeded the legal limit: I am sure the vehicles in our Sunday cavalcades did.

Besides a hugely enjoyed Guy Fawkes Day, the first half of November brought the Chapel's annual Sale of Work. Fortunately — or possibly by design — the dates did not clash, the Sale falling a week or so after bonfire junketings. Its title was pronounced in local speech as 'Saylerwork'. Accordingly, in pre-reading days, I thought it to be 'Sailor Work' and that in some mysterious way Chapel and Royal Navy had together conspired to produce marketable goods. (Knowledge of the Navy had been gleaned from a Christmas present in the shape of a picture book on the Senior Service's wartime deeds). The delusion soon faded on actually attending the event.

The goods on sale were those stitched, machined, knitted, crocheted, embroidered or created by any other method by ladies of the Chapel during the previous twelve months. Pillow and bolster cases, cushion covers, valances, counterpanes, tea cloths, table linen, sheets and so forth, plain and designed, were piled on stalls lining the Sunday School walls. Behind the stalls stood the sales ladies, all hatted, with Grandma among them, and an air of not letting business interfere unduly with an important social occasion. (Proof that sales ladies had eyes and thoughts on matters other than commerce lay in Grandma's ability to recall in exact detail days later who attended and what, if adult female, they were wearing).

Those attending were numerous and not restricted to people of Wesleyan persuasion. And their numbers increased year by year until, in 1924 or '25, the event stretched over three days instead of two: afternoons and evenings Wednesday to Friday inclusive. That it should increase in popularity was not surprising. It was pleasant in those days of few entertainments to step from raw outdoor November into the Sale's milling warmth. A warmth which, indeed, amounted almost to a fug. The hot water pipes were at their considerable hottest, the press of people gave off more heat. Warm air wafted in from side rooms where the large tea-urns of School treat fame did duty, surrounded by mounds of sausage rolls, tarts, scones, cakes, sandwiches and fruit loaf and platters and bowls of trifles and jellies.

The long forms, positioned as for Sunday School, faced the platform ready for the evening concert. The afternoons saw most of the selling and by 5 o'clock a drone of talk filled the School room. Two men sat at a little table near the entrance door taking admission money which was dropped into their waiting sugar basins pinging cheerfully. Visiting ladies fingered materials knowingly. The two resident ministers flitted from group to group carefully avoiding the pitfall of lingering too long with any. A few Chapel elders inhabited the forms this early, armed with steaming cups of tea and sandwiches, likely combining business and social talk. Children munched sausage rolls and cakes and watched people having a lucky dip in a bran tub near to the entrance. Or we wandered to the Band Room to see if anything was happening there. (One year we found a red-haired bank clerk playing "Kitten on the Keys" on the Band Room piano, which was memorable because of being the first time I had *seen* a syncopated piece played).

But for most people the evening concert was the Sale of Work's main attraction. The forms would be almost full by 7 o'clock and, when the local orchestra played its first item soon afterwards, it was usually to a capacity audience. At this time the orchestra could be called the pride of the town. Created by its conductor (a lady whose designatory letters, L.R.A.M., that appeared on handbills and posters, were impressive — to me, anyway), she had welded limited available talent into a commendable unit. For me, the orchestra presented visual entertainment too. The double bass player, eighty odd and craggy visaged as a cliff face, sawing away, The violins, sometimes with one leg outstretched, so wrapt in concentration. And, best of all, the central figure of the conductor on her railed rostrum drawing one's eyes again and again to her arms' continuous movement, a sleeveless gown revealing them as quite beautiful.

Between orchestral items were solo songs and dancing displays by girls of the Wesleyan School. The girls' performances never seemed to go wrong and base spirits were denied looked-for light relief, so well had the troupe been drilled. Singers at my first Sales of Work were locals but their reign ended when the Sale acquired its extra day. They were succeeded by professionals, male and female, from Leeds. Smart in evening clothes and encouraged by large appreciative audiences, they brought us a new vocal standard. And, incidentally, introduced to many of us the delights of Edward German and lovely traditional airs such as "The Ash Grove". Apparently Yorkshire had something to offer in addition to famous cricketers.

NINE : SOME PARTICULAR PLEASURES

"Little things please little minds", the taunt applied to those thought frittering time on childish pursuits, cannot be applicable to young children. They, being small, are entitled to act in accordance with their age. They also dream dreams and experience sensations of touch, scent and secret gratification. And carry recollections of such gratifications undimmed into later life: quaint shadows thrown on a ceiling by flickering firelight before the lamp is lit; the fragrance of honeysuckle at a back door; the curve of a girl's cheek...

We cannot know things so everyday will cling limpet-like to consciousness, so fleeting are they at the time and coming, as they often do, from mundane circumstance. For example, something really mundane — the annual summertime road repairing. It would be heralded by the depositing of neat gravel or flint mounds on footpath and grass verge. Briefly neat, that is, until our thrusting climbing feet, in playing King of the Castle or mountaineers, flattened heap after heap, their edges widening ever more untidily. The almost sensual feel of gravel and flint through thin-soled plimsolls lingers on.

And the actual road repairing, with sweating men ministering to the blackened chimneyed, tar dispensing cauldron on wheels. The stuff would be spread over half a road width, a glistening molten carpet for more sweating men to cover with shovels-full of gravel or flint chippings. Then, finally, the steam-roller, ponderous as an elephant, puffing and crunching and crushing, its driver fittingly majestic. All operations gave pleasure but none was greater than the delicious smell of tar, equalled for me only be the aroma of coffee being ground.

Little things, recollected from long ago, please ageing minds.

Apart from creature comforts, being read to is for many one of the earliest remembered pleasures; certainly it was for me. The house seemed full of books so perhaps a tincture of infant auto-suggestion assisted towards an early liking for the printed word. Coming downstairs you could hardly fail to notice shelves occupying most of the wall above the stairfoot door or an adjoining overflow shelf on one side wall. Facing shelves carried classics — Shakespeare, Scott, *John Halifax, Gentleman* and so on — the side shelf, cheap editions of then popular novels purchased by exiled or soon-to-be-exiled aunts. These included works by A. G. Hales and Gene Stratton Porter and, because of their coloured dust jackets, looked more inviting in spite of cheap rough pages.

But around 1920 personal investigations into what lay under book covers, no matter how seductive the dust jacket, was sometime ahead. In the meantime grown-ups responded nobly to my evening plea, "Will you read to me?" (Grown-ups had a more exacting role in those days: thirty or forty years on, a switched-on television set would obviate, or be thought to obviate, very often the chore of reading to a child). So on most evenings, particularly when dusk fell early, a need for imagery, "being told a story", received its fulfilment. It was the best part of the day. Settled with legs dangling over a chair arm, or knees drawn up to one's chin, gazing unseeing into space but with the mind's eye filled by pictures conjured up in the reading.

First *Rainbow* and *Tiger Tim's Weekly*, which featured the same animal characters. Mrs. Bruin's pupils — Tiger Tim, Jumbo, Bobby Bruin (apparently unrelated to his teacher), Joey the parrot, Willie the ostrich, Georgie Giraffe —paraded realistically, imagination sharpened by the papers' abundant line illustrations. Like all juvenile periodicals, they had a feeling for topicality: snow-topped mastheads around Christmas, firework japes immediately prior to the 5th of November, a mass descent on the seaside by the whole Bruin academy in August. Pictures of the August holiday were puzzling. In the background cliffs loomed, in the foreground a mandatory starfish appeared. At the time, my seaside experience limited to the flat Lincolnshire coast, I had seen neither.

When we, readers and read to, graduated from Tiger Tim & Co to Greyfriars stories cannot be dated precisely. What is certain is that it came about from maternal inspiration on bringing home a copy of the *Magnet* ("... it might be too old for him, but ..."). I would be around eight with sufficient reading skill to manage comics (although evening sessions of being read to were still taking place). The *Magnet* proved a roaring success. For the grown-ups a change to stories aimed at an older age group had a stimulating effect. They, too, relished the antics of Billy Bunter and the Famous Five. Repititious detail — Bunter and his non-existent postal-order, Mr. Quelch's never completed "History of Greyfriars", Lord Mauleverer's fivers, the unvarying slang —were no bars to enjoyment. Indeed they enhanced it like recognised but small and tolerated failings in a beloved.

The author, Frank Richards, by the staggering size of his output and enthralment of several junior generations, attracted serious critical attention from 1940 onwards, originally from no less a figure than George Orwell. The enchantment came, in my view, from an 'other world' cosiness — a marvellously conveyed hedonism of eating hot muffins before a blazing study fire after a hard football game, November rain lashing at the window-panes —and the many unforgettable characters, Billy Bunter above all and undeniably a classic.

The *Magnet* coupled with a gift from a friend of footballer portraits 'presented free' by *Sport and Adventure*, a short lived boys' weekly, stimulated curiosity as to the fount from which such treasures emanated. This would be around 1922, the newsagent/dispenser of the treasures still trading from his original Bridge Street shop. It was a small shop, from the outside humdrum but magical inside. A short ramp led down to a sloping counter that hogged restricted space like a double bed in a boxroom. Mr. Perkins, tall and gingery, usually officiated behind the counter, proprietorial and inclined to tartness when dealing with dawdling small boys. But wariness of receiving a possible discomforting quip gave only the merest check to one's pleasure. The aroma of fresh print rose from the ranks of displayed periodicals heady as a seductive scent. The lurid covers of boys' papers — easily the most numerous — beckoned invitingly.

It was the golden age of boys' weeklies. Two big firms vied for our tuppences. The Amalgamated Press of London had many arrows to its quiver — *Boys' Friend, Boys' Realm, Champion, Union Jack, Football and Sports Favourite, Sports Budget, Magnet,* and its school story companions, *Gem* and *Popular* among them. They were a varied lot in content and format, ranging from World War epics in *Champion* to the long running St. Jim's School yarns in *Gem,* from a mini-broadsheet such as *Boys' Realm* to the compact *Sports Budget.*

Striking uniformity of appearance and content was, however, a hall-mark of the rival Thomson's of Dundee. Thomson's launched *Adventure,* their first boys' weekly in 1921, and followed it the following year with *Rover* and *Wizard.* The trio had an identical format, similar coloured covers, similar adventure and sporting stories, the same illustrators (or so it seemed) whose heroes were remarkably muscled and deep chested.

Thomson's and the Amalgamated Press did not quite have the field to themselves. During these early 'Twenties Allied Newspapers founded the notable *Boys' Magazine.* On Saturdays its small pink covered presence lay among Mr. Perkins's display like a single-coloured flower among many variegated ones. Its featured detective, Falcon Swift, "the monacled manhunter", soon became as famous as Nelson Lee and Sexton Blake, and futuristic fiction at least matched that in rival publications.

Competition among publishers was intense, especially between 1921 and 1924 and, to a lesser extent, up to 1927. They wooed us with so-called free gifts. "FREE WITH EVERY COPY", the covers screamed in large capitals. "A REAL GLOSSY PHOTO OF ..." (usually a prominent sportsman). There were glossy photos of footballers (particularly footballers), cricketers and athletes in head and shoulder, knee length and action poses, monochrome and 'hand coloured'. There were series in sepia and little albums in colour (the latter from Thomson's). There were team groups of county cricket and football clubs of all sizes from no bigger than a cigarette card to octavo; glossy monochrome, glossy coloured, matt plain and matt coloured. And the flood was not restricted to sportsmen. Thomson's, for example, offered "Adventure Pictures" (a few titles: Ambushed by Mexican bandits, Out on the African Veldt, The Canadian Lumber Jack will demonstrate the tone), while the Amalgamated Press issued in 1927 the two Great Wars series. "Heroic Deeds" and "Thrilling Scenes".

Our aggregate tuppences were plainly a prize warranting the dangling of many carrots.

The change to doing all reading alone came unsought by either side. Perhaps it happened in summer when evenings were spent outdoors and, by the time days of shorter daylight returned, an advance to solo ability had been accomplished. Or, impatient to learn of the latest Greyfriars development immediately the *Magnet* arrived, reading skill had burgeoned like force-ripened rhubarb. Again, Miss Credland of Standard 3 had proved an opener of magic casements in introducing us to *Alice in Wonderland* (my first classic). So, too, with poetry. In Standard 2 we had met Wordsworth's daffodils and shared Browning's home thoughts from abroad. Now Miss Credland gave us James Hogg's *A Boy's Song* ("...there's the way for Billy and me"). Somehow Lewis

Carroll and Hogg seemed to merge into an idyllic countryside of deep pools, hazel clad banks and lush meadows peopled by March Hares, talking playing-cards and a perfect companion named Billy.

Demonstrably, then, the printed word was many-sided in attraction, the incentives to explore urgent. Inevitably first essays were boys' papers. It naturally followed that the *Magnet's* companion weeklies *Gem* and *Popular*, would be sampled when opportunity arose. Similarities did strike one — for instance, all three schools (Greyfriars, St. Jim's and Rookwood) had leading characters who were either fat or of noble birth (for example, Bunter of Greyfriars and Arthur Augustus D'Arcy of St. Jim's). But nobody guessed the authors — Frank Richards in *Magnet*, Martin Cifford in *Gem* and Owen Conquest in *Popular* — were, in fact, one and the same man, Charles Hamilton. His annual output was said to be a staggering million and a half words. Kept up for a period of over thirty years his career can be seen as amazing.

A burning interest in football led to a regular perusal of *Football and Sports Favourite*, which lasted most of the decade. The "... and Sports" in the title was actually a courtesy addendum as only a rare cricket serial in summer or a still rarer Rugby League (never Rugby Union) serial in autumn and winter interrupted the flow of soccer fiction. This fiction had its own conventions with differing emphasis placed on one part or other of a story line to give some semblance of variation. A typical story went like this. A young centre-forward aged 19 (invariably 19 which was apparently thought an ideal age for readership identification) signed for an ailing club. After several adversities, which could be dealing with a corrupt manager and hostile teammates, he would emerge triumphant, his goals saving the club and, incidentally, winning the hand of a director's daughter (who had stuck by him throughout) after a chaste courtship. The *Favourite*, aimed at an older age group, differed from the Thomson papers, for whom girls did not exist, and other Amalgamated Press weeklies such as *Champion*, where the fair sex received scant mention. The *Favourites's* authors' styles were recognisable. C. Malcolm Hincks could never be mistaken for Arthur S. Hardy even without a byline, while in addition Stanton Hope hit on a variation in subject matter. He featured a Royal Navy team led by one, Hookey Walker, which was attached to a ship seemingly permanently anchored off Southsea.

These authors also wrote for the *Favourite's* companion weekly, *Sports Budget*, which, apart from a few short articles, consisted of a long complete story and an instalment of a serial. During my irregular perusals, the serial mostly concerned the adventures of Peter Wild, a film star who could perform wonders on any sports arena. Like the *Favourite*, *Sports Budget* concentrated on professional football as a blackcloth for its fiction, a fiction that had evolved its own clichés. For instance, when a strong shot beat a goalkeeper, a phrase 'the rigging bulged' was used time and again. The papers' editors may have undergone a course on P. G. Wodehouse for they addressed correspondents in print as 'old fruit', 'old sport' and the like. And articles on footballers were much given to plays on words — "Tom's a half-back but there are no half-measures about his play", "...now wears Glasgow Rangers' light blue. And it's the fellows who oppose him who are in the blues — deep blues, too".

Boys' Magazine, that rogue elephant among Amalgamated Press and Thomson herds, also included much soccer fiction, to the extent (if memory serves) of Falcon Swift taking the role — brilliantly, of course — of a demon centre-forward in the execution of some detective duty. On analysis we find these detectives of boys' weeklies had their own conventions. Take nomenclature. They had unusual first names of two syllables and fairly common surnames of one — Sexton Blake, Nelson Lee, Falcon Swift, Dixon Hawke, Ferrers Locke — thus imitating their probable source, Sherlock Holmes. They employed boy assistants for the readership to identify with. Sometimes those assistants were apparently devoid of a surname (Blake's Tinker, Lee's Nipper). Sometimes they had scholastic links: Locke was a cousin of Dr. Locke, Headmaster of Greyfriars, Nelson Lee a housemaster at St. Frank's. The St. Frank's stories were as readable as those so prolifically turned out by Charles Hamilton, and the work of Edwy Searles Brooks who also, among many divers hands, wrote Sexton Blake stories for *Union Jack*.

Richmal Crompton's *William* books were among the first, if not the very first, hardbacks devoured. Introduction came early in that delectable scamp's long career, perhaps even in the year of his launching, 1922. Discovering *William* equalled that of discovering Greyfriars. Thoughtful relatives gave *William* books at present giving times and an aunt was apt to leave copies of *Happy Mag* behind after weekend visits. *Happy Mag*, a monthly light fiction miscellany typical of the 'Twenties, published single *William* episodes.

By fairly general consent *William* is reckoned a major comic character of twentieth century fiction. He was not specifically aimed at children by his creator. This had a valuable side effect as one's vocabulary was being enlarged and understanding stretched, and so great the pleasure you were unaware of imbibing 'education'.

William combined in his scruffy eleven-year-old person, though in extreme form, the boyhood feelings that grown-ups are oppressive, girls soppy (but only for most of the time) and rumpled comfort infinitely preferable to starched elegance. His faithful mongrel, Jumble, possessed all the endearing doggy virtues; his gang, the Outlaws — Ginger, Henry and Douglas — proven ideal aides. These factors stayed in mind, uniform parts of a perfectly conceived whole. And so, just as strongly, did William's world. What a world it was. Vaguely Home Counties sited, suburban yet pastoral, inhabited by eccentric artists, peppery pensioned-off military gentlemen and cat adoring spinsters — boy haters to a man or woman mostly. A family composed of a long suffering father either working in some undefined office or at home immersed in the City pages of his newspaper, a mother possessing Job's patience, an elder brother and sister with interests limited to tennis, amateur theatricals and chaste superficial love affairs and a domestic staff of two, as long suffering in their way as Mr. Brown.

The original Thomas Henry illustrations are as inseparable from Richmal Crompton's text as is the work of Tenniel from Lewis Carroll's. William, cap askew on a mop of unbrushed hair, slack tie under a partly turned down collar, jacket and shorts the worse for wear, stockings wrinkled, shoes scuffed

OUT ON THE AFRICAN VELDT

AMBUSHED BY MEXICAN BANDITS

To My Fellow Readers
Sincerely
Harry Langdon

HARRY LANGDON—A FIRST NATIONAL STAR

and mud caked — an epitome of the juvenile primitive.

Other than sports pages — devotedly scanned if not always fully understood — the *Daily Chronicle* offered nothing to interest an eight- or nine-year old reader. When the pages were flicked through columns of solid print looked intimidating indeed. Even advertisements tended to be wordy and smudgy photographs were short commons after, say, Heath Robinson's ingenious drawings in my *Playbox Annual*. The *Chronicle's* back page, regularly seen as its inside carried football matter, was specially fearsome. Seven columns covering Sales by Auction, Properties for Sale, Properties Wanted, Businesses for Sale and Situations Vacant, all in the tiniest print imaginable. Very daunting!

In contrast the local paper at this time began to merit attention. By supper time on Fridays all adults appeared to know everything that the day's local rag had reported or opined. ('Local rag', the term adopted country wide these many years for a district newspaper, was in our case at least tinged with affection). There is no difficulty in pinpointing reasons for a local newspaper's appeal. It is, above all, cosy. By addressing a comparative few it can generate a warmth many people, consciously or no, feel is lacking in a national organ. It is in a real sense 'theirs', the readers, bringing tidings of the dear known scene and people — particularly people. Implanted on every local editor's and reporter's psyche must be the truism, "Everybody likes reading about themselves and people they know".

My thinking of the local organ as 'our paper' received a fillip with a tenuous knowledge of its manufacture. The printing works lay over that stretch of river flanking the approach road to the Wesleyan School. In a few minutes you could nip round via the Town bridge, drawn on Thursdays by the sound of machinery

114

going flat out. (Thursdays saw most of the edition printed and the completed papers arrived on newsagents' counters the following afternoon). The works door had glass panels through which its ground floor could be seen. Wheels spun, belts rotated, parts moved. Such a clanking and whirring and grinding and vibrating. The floor shook, a smell of printing ink filtered through to the street. To a child from an industrial area the scene would not have presented anything extraordinary, but we rustics, if not exactly spellbound, were assuredly impressed.

The paper consisted of two broadsheets (i.e. four pages) where the lay out remained constant for many years. The front page's left-hand column carried small classified advertisements — Wanted, Lost and Found, Situations Vacant etc — this last revealing a fair traffic in domestics. "Experienced generals" especially were in short supply. Situations Vacant gave womenfolk a deal of interest ("I see Mrs Mallinson's wantin' a general agen — she niver could keep one for long"). The rest of the front page was devoted to trade advertisements with a stone mason's central position made more prominent by a gravestone photograph starkly white on a black background. The cinema's weekly programme always occupied page 2's top left-hand corner (its Spa rival similarly occupied page 4's). Page 2 also had the leader and a string of paragraphs on local affairs — some notable leaving the town, preachers for Sunday's services, shops' and post office's opening hours during a holiday period, a Primrose League meeting. Page 3 encompassed the issue's meat: long near-verbatim reports of Council and Tradesmens' Association meetings, police court proceedings, the more important weddings and funerals. The back page gave the Spa news, local sport and, in the final column 'Coming Events' stretching four or five months ahead: jumble sales, dances, whist drives, garden fêtes, flag days, flower shows. This column also squeezed in the Territorial Platoon's weekly orders, meteorological readings, lighting-up times and lastly, as if to give readers a parting reminder of life's eternal verities, Births, Marriages and Deaths.

Around 1920 we of the small fry fraternity were dimly aware of a miraculous new invention called wireless. Except for one manifestation, no tangible evidence of its existence could be seen locally. But we knew the word 'wireless' presupposed it worked with little or no gadgetry, rather resembling a Good Fairy waving her magic wand. At the same time the local manifestation was very tangible indeed. On the town's southern outskirts three masts towered over their owner's largish villa, apparently tethered by many stout cables. From the Wong (from which viewpoint they were usually seen) their triangular patterns dominated the skyline like a giant schooner's sails on a seascape. What results our pioneer achieved had not, so far as I know, been recorded. He was famous also as a spiritualist so perhaps he got sounds both spiritual and worldly.

The populace had an opportunity — in most cases a first opportunity — to 'listen in' at the August Bank Holiday gala shortly after BBC stations started functioning. A board at a marquee entrance advertised a few minutes' listening-in at sixpence a time. This was a price high enough to ensure no customer had to wait unduly long for his turn. On entering you were immediately impressed. The banked equipment had such a profusion of dials and knobs and coils and valves and (so much for the word 'wireless'!) wires. These men must be very clever to work it, you thought. "This is all the way from Newcastle," said one of them jovially as he placed headphones over my expectant ears. Newcastle! I could pinpoint that city on my school atlas far to our north and, more importantly, lots of cigarette and boys' periodical cards featured footballers in Newcastle United's famous black and white livery. A woman singer could be heard over the headphones, a piercing soprano. There were lots of crackles and a kind of low hissing like bacon sizzling. But it was wonderful: a woman singing up in Newcastle and hearing her one hundred and forty miles away!

After this introduction there was a lull in the town respecting further developments. Then, in 1924, came an explosion. Aerials became part of the scene in backyards and gardens — poles, as tall as or taller than the houses, placed a goodly distance away and carrying a thickish cable to chimney stacks. For a time local suppliers enjoyed brisk business in erecting these monster clothes lines, as a wag called them.

Our first set was acquired that autumn and started operating one Saturday, as I recall. On the way to the cinema matinée that afternoon I met Mr. Turner and his assistant. They were pushing a handcart on which lay an overlapping pole, a long ladder, a tool bag and a coil of cable. "Your aerial," Mr. Turner sang out, as if I didn't know. I returned two and a half hours later to find his work done and an expansive Mr. Turner sat in our Kitchen supping a cup of strong tea like the good fellow Wesleyan he was. (Thinking back, we appeared to patronise Wesleyan tradesmen exclusively with one exception — Uncle George, Grandad's boot repairer brother. But he was 'family'). Our newly erected pole stood firmly by the second clothes post, suspended cable encircled the chimney stack, the Kitchen window frame had been pierced to take aerial and earth wires, the latter attached externally to an old poker stuck into ground adjoining a wallflower bed. A new era had begun.

It was a crystal set, a yellowy coloured wooden box on whose black top stood the cat's whisker encapsulated with its crystal. A small attached board that had two rows of points on to which headphone leads were screwed allowed several people to listen at the same time. I found headphones something of a trial after twenty minutes or so unless the programme held one. But this might have been a ten-year-old's fidgets for, conversely, Grandma's staying power was considerable. At nearly seventy her appetite for a new pastime waxed undiminished.

Nonetheless, two years later she replaced the crystal set with a valve set and horn type loudspeaker. "Everybody can listen now," Grandma said, organising a re-deployment of furniture (the dresser relegated to the back kitchen, a small bamboo table introduced to accommodate the new set and other furniture shifted around). The new set certainly brought improvements — a less finicky tuning and no imprisoning headphones. And, with the loudspeaker holding forth to all and sundry, programme patterns and content crept unbidden into consciousness in a way impossible in crystal set days. There were no dance music broadcasts on Sundays, the lightest fare coming from the

Grand Hotel, Eastbourne, in the shape of Albert Sandler and his orchestra —Grandma's favourite programme. Ordinary days brought their own longueurs. Seemingly interminable shipping forecasts and a recital of minority information entitled Fat Stock Prices in which hoggets and shearlings eventually made a couplet refrain as inseparable in one's mind as brimstone and treacle or nuts and bolts. And an evening series, Foundations of Music, that went on so many years; long enough, you felt, to have seen the foundations of a thousand cathedrals. We ranked the series only a rung above abhorred chamber music (which may show a sad musical philistinism but we knew what we liked).

What we liked were variety programmes, billed under the pleasant sounding title of Vaudeville; especially comedians from those 'made' by radio (John Henry and Blossom, and Stainless Stephens for example) to those long famous (George Robey, Sir Harry Lauder). A Lauder broadcast was, indeed, to Grandma — and to Grandad, although rather less so — an event. In Grandma's affections, Lauder's song "Keep right on to the end of the road" ousted our gramophone record of "Where my caravan has rested". I must confess to being somewhat lukewarm towards these established music hall stars and, perhaps in compensation, became the household's greatest enthusiast for Charlot's Hour. André Charlot, then a West End celebrity, had concocted a mélange of sketch and song light as thistledown. It was deemed the height of 1927 radio sophistication and, if he had known, M. Charlot might have viewed the approbation of a thirteen-year-old with rather mixed feelings. But by then a steady diet of adult reading matter had bred a certain precocity.

Given this taste, it is not surprising that dance bands, propagators of newest and most trendy music, were listened to on every permitted occasion. Here too a preference pecking order developed — Ambrose, Fred Elizalde, Alfredo from the New Princes Restaurant and the Savoy bands, Orpheans and Havana. Of these, Elizalde ranked first purely on his own piano playing, producing enchanting effects undreamt of hitherto. A side effect of devoted listening gave young people a familiarity with new tunes impossible before radio's advent. This in turn encouraged the one shop selling sheet music to fill a window with latest hits and to keep its wares up to date, a turnabout from not long before when, say, "Pasadena" could hold pride of place indefinitely. Not only dance bands played these tunes. The cinema organ (whose players curiously seemed mostly to rejoice in the first name of Reginald) also had frequent broadcasts, thundering them out in every conceivable Wurlitzian effect.

The book, *In Search of England*, published in 1927, describes how the author, H. V. Morton, heard the wireless in an old Cornish farmhouse during the previous year. On the walls portraits of Queen Victoria and Field Marshal Kitchener looked down on the listeners. A band from the Savoy Hotel played, a buzz of talk and a tinkling of glasses could be heard. The listeners were completely absorbed. The scene, I know, was typical.

Going with a grown-up to the cinema's evening performance was a highly circumspect affair in no way comparable to Saturday afternoon anarchy. With shops shuttered for an hour past, pedestrians' footsteps echoed in quiet streets.

If after dark you chanced upon few loiterers, these inevitably on the Town bridge or under the big street lamp opposite the cinema entrance.

Unlike Saturday matinées, a full complement of retainers awaited evening patrons. One of them stood well down the aisle level with the last row of sixpennies, his job to ensure sixpenny patrons occupied the forms immediately fronting the screen (our Saturday matinée territory). He had little trouble before the performance began but afterwards, when lights dimmed, malefactors were wont to illegally transfer to the more advantageously placed ninepennies.

Unless forestalled by earlier arrivals we went to the same spot: the last right-hand ninepenny row. (I realise now a happy medium between the impecunious sixpennies and plutocrats in balcony one-and-threes). Actually our 'row' was a long undivided well-padded seat which possessed a comfortably curved back. Its greater comfort outweighed an increased likelihood of a blocked view — the hall did not have the slope found in purpose built cinemas.

About 7.25 the pianist went to his instrument, then positioned at floor level under the screen. He walked purposefully puffing a pipe, shoulders slightly hunched and undoubtedly aware of his major part in the proceedings. Promptly at 7.30 main lights were switched off, the projector wheels whirred, its beam cutting through the darkness and holding a haze of spiralling tobacco smoke as images appeared on the screen. The show had begun.

Usually the show contained four items: an instalment of a serial, a two-reel comedy, a newsreel and 'the big picture'. In addition there might be a magazine-type feature, such as Pathé Pictorial, showing events like Hollywood stars' bathing parties and fashion parades whose preening mannequins drew loud sniggers and occasional catcalls from darkness-emboldened youths. But these were a bonus. While supporting films maintained a fair consistency, the big pictures — generally a six-reeler — gave varying amounts of pleasure to a small boy. Often grown-ups knew for certain they would be entertained (Grandma, for example, knew any film with Henry Edwards or Matheson Lang in the cast would please her). Probably limited understanding made a child's pleasure more chancy.

But memory retains even some big pictures not especially enjoyed at the time. The first Dr. Mabuse film, because a series of cards akin to cigarette cards were issued from the box office weeks before its showing. *The Lost Chord* for the fact a local soprano sang the title song during the performance. *In a Monastery Garden* for a like reason, the panatrope blasting out the theme tune several times during a film emotional enough to satisfy the most sentimental. And of course ones remembered with affection — the de Mille biblical epics, Chaplin and Harold Lloyd full length comedies, *The Four Horsemen of the Apocalypse*.

Come a quarter to ten and we who had stood when the lights went up while the pianist played the national anthem, would emerge under the gaze of those youths who had spilled out immediately 'The End' flashed on the screen. They stood under the big lamp opposite: quite silent, cigarettes in mouth corners, hands in trouser pockets. And starting that long, evaluating, absorbed Lincolnshire stare before slowly departing for home or fish and chip shop.

118

By around 1928, no matter how mediocre the programme, it was worthwhile going to the cinema just to hear a young pianist who had recently taken over. Circumstances sometimes conspire to maximise receptivity to a new experience. It happened now. His brilliant interpretations of popular melodies on a resonant instrument ideally suited to the hall's acoustics coupled with one's current stage of development, opened ears to new delights.

Syncopated piano playing had moved on from war years' ragtime and subsequent Zez Confrey-like tinkling novelties to a fuller bodied sophistication. This much was clear to anyone who avidly listened to Elizalde, Mayerl, Carroll Gibbons and others on the wireless. Such masters treated an anaemic sixpenny song sheet version — which humble amateurs played 'as written' —as a mere skeleton to be built on.

So did our young pianist. With an admirable technique allied to a formidable knowledge of harmony and chordal structure, he produced sounds otherwise heard only through a wireless loudpseaker. Later opportunities to actually see those nimble fingers in action were eagerly grasped. Seeing the left hand's effortless mastery of forward and back tenth, orthodox after-beat and cunning variations of rhythm. And the right hand's big four- and five-finger chords interspersed with connecting single note breaks and endless experimentation with Mayerl-like runs of fourths and subtly introduced chromatic sevenths and ninths. It was sheer magic.

The melodies he played, then lifted brand new from the radio, are played still these many decades later as 'standards' or 'evergreens'. The fast, exuberant "Variety Drag" and "Miss Annabelle Lee" for example, the first happily coinciding with a local showing of *The Collegians*, a serial based on American university life which we thought the ultimate in modernity. The slower "Mean to Me", "A Cottage for Sale", "She's funny that way", "Body and Soul" and the waltzes "Pagan Love Song" and Noel Coward's "I'll see you again".

His piano cut through all distractions — an audibly whirring projector, any buzz of talk — transporting one to a kind of faraway land, vague, even translucent, but lovely. It was conjured from cascading, modulating sound, making you wistful or fulfilled, content or a touch sad in turn.

Never were intermissions for the screening of dull advertisements so anticipated and relished. The lyric to one of his pieces went "The song is ended, but the melody lingers on ..." It does still.

TEN : GOING PLACES

In one sense the title of this chapter is a misnomer because travelling to distant places was what the majority rarely, sometimes never, did. Other than fortunates with generous regulated holidays, such as teachers and bank personnel, the employed might get a brief week's leave in addition to statutory bank holidays. But, as noted before, money was short and simply did not run to the charges of seaside boarding houses. As for self-employed small shopkeepers and trades-men, most of them could not afford to close their businesses for days on end.

Yet there was no feeling of deprivation, of missing out. The locals' oft-used "what you've nivver 'ed, y' nivver miss" fitted perfectly their cheerful resignation to life's little omissions. What had been good enough for their parents was good enough for them. So long as they had a roof over their heads, warmth and sufficient food they saw no point in repining: no bad philosophy and one that certainly made for contentment.

Many older people, too, positively disliked going away. Grandad was typical in this. Up at 6.30, in bed by 10, his meal times inflexibly on the dot —although by no means an unreasonable man, any departure from the daily norm bothered him. How much more worrying, therefore, a necessity to don tie and best suit, to leave for days the surroundings familiar over forty years.

Times, however, were changing. The coming of the buses in the 'Twenties brought a new mobility, wireless and cinema new, exciting dimensions to life.

The ubiquitous bicycle. Although it is impossible to measure precisely, perhaps half the population rode a bicycle at some time every ordinary weekday. Mounts ranged from ancient to the then modern. Riders came from all age and social groups — old, young and middle-aged, artisans and professional men, housewives and shop girls. A working man would talk about 'me owd grid' in tones revealing wry affection and pride in ownership. Possessing it enabled him to get home for a reasonably leisurely midday meal whereas walking would have meant a rushed one. And this, in fine, showed what for most the cycle conferred: a means of quickly moving between two points within the town's square mile. True, schoolboys such as M and me cycled longest distances visiting out-of-town form cronies (Sugar at Moorhouses, Alan Blackburn and Freddy Belton at Coningsby, Jack Goodrick at Tumby Woodside), but this was exceptional. To our elders, such 'spins' (as bike rides were then called) indicated a need to dissipate youthful energy and/or the enjoyment of owning new cycles. Cycling for pleasure did not in my day assume mass appeal until the 1930s. Then, on Sundays, cycling clubs swept through the town bound for or returning from the coast, alpaca jacketed and in corduroy shorts, crouched over their handlebars and closely bunched.

Before, whether or not long rides were undertaken, no doubts existed in boys' minds as to the most desirable model. The one with fully dropped handlebars and narrow tyres — a 'racing bike' — which so patently exuded speed and intimations of derring-do. Really there were no other candidates though semi-dropped handlebars were acceptable (and, truth to tell, more comfortable for mundane purpose). How different these light, attractively rakish steeds from other types. Particularly so from the red Post Office monster a postman neighbour had daily to flog round the hilly Wold district of Belchford and Scambleby. Built for long life, great weight made greater by a mail bag in its carrier over the front wheel, it typified G.P.O. officialdom.

Not so heavy but distinctly solid were the bicycles used by our upper crust. These tended to have their chains encased and, of course, always had handlebars of maximum uprightness. The riders somehow achieved a splendid dignity. A couple of examples leap instantly to mind. The vicar went his rounds imperially yet benignly, a little smile hovering, rosy cheeks aglowing. And the formidable spinster from Louth Road, middle-aged and buxom, whose large teeth were bared even when not smiling. She rode as a queen might have ridden — bolt upright and regal of mien.

As easily recalled: the acrid smell of the carbide lamp which after lighting-up times pervaded highway and byway with a pungency worthy of our leather works.

Because of geography trains could not present to the populace so obvious a travelling symbol as the ever more common motor bus. The station stood lonely on the town's western edge, a modest outpost yet possessing, for us who journeyed seldom, a faintly romantic aura. You took the left fork where West Street bisected. A little way ahead the station lay, its approach rising flint-paved ground beyond a wide four-barred gate.

Besides the intangible romantic the station had that air of permanence Victorian solidity bestows. The main building had two storeys, the upper forming the station master's living quarters, betokened by window blinds with crochet-work bottoms. The lower, pierced midway by a through lobby to the platform, contained doors to booking and goods offices and the little arched window through which tickets were issued. Opposite the ticket window stood a hefty weighing machine and, just inside the lobby entance, a vending machine that dispensed penny bars of Nestlé's chocolate. Both machines fully maintained their environment's atmosphere. As in the case of the postman's bicycle, each and every object had to be of maximum weight.

Before entering the lobby other arresting things could be taken in. A substantial goods warehouse projected from one end of the main building, a huge door above its loading ramp almost accounting for one side. A rail track led from the ramp across the station yard and it would have been momentous to have chanced upon a wagon on these rails. But now they appeared to be totally disused and the ramp served merely to load a horse drawn dray that delivered goods and parcels locally. The yard boasted other structures, of recent origin and indicative of changing times. They belonged to a small petrol depot. Sited near the riverside boundary well away from the station, these horizontal cylindrical tanks were as modern a portent as our sprouting wireless aerials.

For most of the 'Twenties the same station master ruled, grey beard and moustache ever in the same state of clipped neatness, ever dapper in gold braided peaked cap and navy blue uniform (and just as dapper in navy serge as a pillar of our Chapel on Sundays). His signalmen were distinguished from the porters by their wearing of 'civilian' cloth caps instead of the glossy-peaked issue, a distinction repeated by goods warehousemen.

Apart from the petrol depot's advent, probably little had changed about the station in its sixty years' existence. Notice boards, on which timetables were pasted, carried the metal lettered headpiece G.N.R. years after the great 1923 railway amalgamations constituted an embracing L.N.E.R. Sheet metal advertisements clamped to yard boundary palings, baldly announcing "Oxo" or succinctly "Virol For Anaemic Girls" and the like, if not original fixtures certainly had rust sufficient to show they had long been there. The famous John Hassall poster, "Skegness Is So Bracing", adorned station approaches more often than not, and maybe had since its original 1909 unveiling. Its portly old salt, gambolling as one inspired, was almost as much part of the station scene as the after-mentioned Red Lion omnibus.

The proprietor of the Red Lion, a commercial hotel, and the local rating officer shared a distinction in that both were habitually referred to by their initials. said so and so..." By long usage the initials had become as inseparable from the two gentlemen as the prominent roles they played in town affairs. Perhaps nobody outside their immediate circles could have told you what E. N. and W. O. stood for and, like mature offspring, the initials had taken on characters of their own. This state of affairs was helped by their names often coming before the public in print. Both were mentioned frequently in local newspapers. Additionally 'W. O. Chapman' appeared in heavy type at the bottom of official notices and six-monthly rate demands. 'E. N. Ashton' was emblazoned on the Red Lion frontage hardly less prominently than the hotel sign itself. And on the town's most familiar vehicle, the horse-drawn hotel omnibus, Red Lion and proprietor had a mobile advertisement in less spectacular lettering.

As I recall, two Red Lion omnibuses operated throughout the decade and beyond until 'progress' supervened. First there was a primrose yellow vehicle presumably superannuated and then one painted deep mahogany in a brilliant sheen. However, the vehicle design did not change nor did its driver. Even after motor-buses became commonplace, people still called it 'The Bus'. It met every train, a sqaure topped, round bottomed box on wheels, but not uncomely. The loftily placed driving seat caused the driver's head and shoulders to protrude well above a roof edged by a shallow rail that prevented luggage sliding off. The driver had a grandly commanding frontal view. He seemed as enduring as the hills, a serious, heavy jowled man crowned with a cap centrally placed and quite unslanted. It also seemed unimaginable for anyone else to drive the Bus, so much a part was he. With feet planted firmly on his sloping footboard, large hands holding reins not too tightly, whip handy should the horse deviate from a normal gentle canter, he can now be seen as a last representative of a vanishing era.

Riding in the Bus had a charm only slightly tempered by crossing town so conspicuously. (The bus did not just ply between station and Red Lion, but could be hired by all comers). Charm evolved from the rarity of being so conveyed and the sheer lulling pleasantness of the Bus's motion. One settled on welcoming upholstery, familiar streets and familiar faces slipped by, the horse's clip-clopping beat a refrain "Home again!" All too short the mile journey felt, yet how cheap at half-a-crown or so.

No impression of leaving an urban centre occurred when the little two-coach train left our terminus. On the right-hand side beyond a malt house the land rose greenly to an appreciable height. To the left all that was visible of the town crouched several fields distant. It looked insignificant, devoid of the bubbling child life one knew. From the huddle you could pick out the Wesleyan Day School turret, the black painted rear of a West Street grain warehouse and, inevitably, the church. But in a trice these tallest points had shrunk to a blur.

For a mile and a half the line ran due south through lush fields bordering the old canal. Canal locks, ironwork rusting and timber decaying, slipped past. Then, after going under Martin bridge, the country changed as the train veered south-west. We puffed up a cutting and on both sides moorland appeared, aflame in summer with purple heather and yellow gorse. (And apt to be literally aflame in dry summers when sparks from a locomotive started fires that scorched and blackened acres, threatening the golf course presaging our approach to the Spa station). Backs of large red brick houses loomed into view, trees there were in abundance — silver birch and pine chiefly — and the train grated to a hissing halt.

A few minutes and off again. This time to go a mere mile side by side with a street that was a perfect example of Victorian ribbon development, and the Junction was reached. "All change!", the porters called, for here the branch line ended and began. Here, you felt, an outgoing journey really started, the gateway to North and South. It was not an imposing gateway, perched on the Witham's banks, open to winds blowing unchecked over flat riverside country. But it served. Long trains steaming in, sometimes disgorging anglers from faraway Sheffield, were harbingers of a quicker world that lay outside our customary ken.

Carriers and their carts were still extant in the 1920s. They plied between villages and neighbouring towns, as they had done for generations, bringing people and produce to market. Each Saturday a prime specimen from the Wold village of Hagworthingham trundled down Spilsby Road, passing our house around 11 a.m. The cart had a roof and enclosed sides, fancifully putting me in mind of a famous Hollywood silent film *The Covered Wagon*. The horse always moved at the same gentle amble, the carrier holding slack reins, always pensive in aspect. A swarthy man of indeterminate age, he wore a black cap and dark clothes, the jacket buttoned to his chin. It never failed to cause one faint surprise on seeing his small, slightly bent figure walking in the town. Like the station omnibus driver he seemed inseparable from his vehicle.

But the age of carriers' carts was nearly over. Already around 1921 we were travelling to Cleethorpes by motor bus, albeit slowly and uncomfortably. The vehicle was a long crate on wheels painted a lugubrious black. Passengers sat on hard seats which ran down the sides in two facing rows, having entered through a door at the back. This door had an open window and fumes wafted in from a long exhaust pipe that protruded below the body. Temporary relief came ten miles out at Cawkwell hill. Its incline was too much for bus and load so bus and driver alone zigzagged to the summit while passengers trudged uphill on foot.

Bus travel had become a deal more comfortable by the middle of the decade when regular services began to operate. As a natural route centre, the town at once became a bus centre with the fleet of our local entrepreneur most in evidence. His had been the second town garage to open, this in itself a departure as he had previously worked as a blacksmith in a nearby village. Now his autumn-brown buses ran to half a dozen coastal and inland places, employing a dozen or more drivers with maintenance staff to match.

Later another local concern started a service to Lincoln using a different route, continuing to operate it for upwards of forty years. From outside chocolate coloured Louth-based buses shared Market Place stands with town companies, providing services south and homewards. In summer bright blue Bray buses from Lincoln, big red Trent and pale yellow East Midlands from Nottingham and Derby plus a miscellany of other buses and char-a-bancs hared through the town coastwards or homeward bound. And, most significantly, several villages had their own village-based bus which replaced the old time carrier's cart.

The bus epoch had arrived.

I understand the town's first garage opened for business in 1906. Standing back a little way from a riverside road, it had probably not changed much in the intervening years. Tall open doors, set at an angle to the road, revealed a spaciousness that must have been over generous in pre-1914 days. Fronting the garage and abutting the pavement, an attached shop offered, beside car components, cycles and gramophones and their accessories. Perhaps this eye for diversity explains the garage's survival in days when motor-cars were not numerous. This pioneer proprietor did not, however, branch out with buses as did the man next to open a garage. But the bus enterprise occurred some years after the latter had taken his strategic site in West Street.

Post-war days saw the real garage mushrooming — three in our road alone during the 'Twenties. First a house outbuilding obligingly jutting end-to-road had a long door inserted and a petrol pump installed outside. The man responsible, Mr. Young, had migrated here on retirement (amazingly *from* Sutton-on-Sea!). He pottered around clad in an oil-smeared, knee length, khaki coloured foreman's coat and his wire-framed spectacles made him look rather like a boffin happily indulging a hobby. (Which perhaps he was). Mr. Young employed an assistant who later started hs own business further towards town in the traction-engine proprietor's yard.

Between the two openings a more momentous one occurred in 1924 with the erection of the town's first post-war purpose built garage. It stood a short fifty yards from our house and one accordingly watched it progress from foundations to completion with an almost possessive interest. New buildings were rare enough but one such as this, symbolising the march of progress, held a special fascination. At dusk the globes on the petrol pumps glowed like pale moons and even when in bed and unable to see them, the garage's dynamo could be heard pulsing away. Its staccato beat seemed to be intoning "Up-to-date" over and over again.

Generally local folk heroes emanated from the ranks of sportsmen, chiefly footballers and, with them, especially performers in the glamorous goal scoring positions. There were others who achieved a lingering fame — for prodigious beer drinking, say, or siring a child when past seventy. These however, though gossip worthy, could not strictly be so classified. Seldom also was it for a trade or occupation to confer folk hero status. Bricklaying and plumbing and tailoring might have a certain cachet but not the necessary charisma. It had to be something manual (sedentary jobs were to many, probably most, effete) and preferably newly emerged.

Bus drivers met these conditions quite admirably. Theirs was a new calling, they were demonstrably manually employed and, moreover, employed in connection with recent technology, the internal combustion engine. And, importantly, they were well paid by depressed mid-Lincolnshire standards.

These symbols of a new calling enjoyed their role to the full. They would park their buses on allotted Market Place spaces and then congregate in a group until departure time, usually cigarette smoking, the cynosure for many eyes. These were the days before the company take-over that enforced the wearing of uniform. In the 'Twenties young drivers were as often as not those with the more rakishly angled caps, among the first to grow sideburns. They knew everybody on the routes. Country folk on being picked up and addressed by name almost genuflected with pleasure. A driver's characteristics were affectionately noted. How Reg curled his tall frame octopus-like round the steering wheel, one arm encircling it as if to engender warmth. How Albert had a quip for all even when sorely tried by fog, frost and snow. How George and Jim, the oldest hands, gave older folk confidence although considered by the young a touch cautious. How another made successful conquests of older women.

Drivers' talk too — of gears and clutches and big ends and breakdowns and timetables — had such an exciting modern flavour. And buses' idiosyncrasies assumed weighty import in their discussions — the undue vibrations of the Dennis, the Leyland's performance in second gear, the Chev's way with hills. Heady talk all of it, redolent of the new age.

To us Lincoln was a metropolis, a centre of sophistication, a dispenser of every imaginable diversion. To our neighbour, Mrs. Cooper, it had proved terrifying also, as she recounted one day. A small stout woman, raven hair scrimped back into a tight little bun, she adopted her usual stance. This consisted of settling back on the heels of her flat shoes, hands over a stomach thus considerably distended. Mrs. Cooper could be taken as a fairly typical Lincolnshire country woman — mother of seven now all grown up, grandmother of an unidentified number of grandchildren, she was goodhearted and honest as the day.

She itemised reasons for disquiet on her (apparently only) visit to Lincoln —too many people, noise, traffic — obvious complaints from one accustomed

125

HIGH STREET SHOWING
THE STONEBOW, LINCOLN

MONKS ROAD, LINCOLN.

CASTLE HILL, LINCOLN.

A Clements' concert party audience circa 1921.

Promenade and shelters, Mablethorpe.

128

A Present from Skegness.

to sounds no more trying than a barking dog or Mr. Cooper chopping firewood. At the end came the gem that made her story memorable: "Wot really may-ed me frit was them 'arzez cummin' dowen the street". ("What really made me frightened were those houses coming down the street"). The mobile houses were trams.

Lincoln trams were limited to High Street — admittedly a long thoroughfare — on a mere 1.83 miles of track. They ran between the busy Stonebow end and Bracebridge, clanking over two level crossings en route, the aspect getting less and less commercial as Bracebridge was reached.

The Stonebow was said to be the county's leading shopping centre. (What shop proprietors in Grimsby's Freeman Street thought about this claim has not, so far as I know, been recorded). Like water eddying around boulders, Saturday shoppers had to thread their way round knots of chatting best-suited men whose ruddy complexions and broad dialect proclaimed them as the farming fraternity. They never appeared to be moved on: the City Police, likewise Lincolnshire men and true, were doubtless tolerant of habitual native standing, staring and talking.

Woolworth's opening circa 1924 brought a new shopping dimension for citizens and out-of-towners alike. A prime High Street site opposite the Picture House coupled with the novelty of a cheap walk-round store ensured milling weekend crowds. "Nothing In This Store Over 6d" ran the famous slogan, and it was undeniably true. Even a small boy who disliked shopping —or at any rate as a tagging-along appendage of a shopping adult — was smitten. And, at those prices, able to make a considered purchase. There were pencils and rubbers and drawing paper and so much more in alluring array and, most alluring of all, books. I wonder how many of my generation acquired a taste for book buying at Woolly's. The store had its own series of unexpurgated and abridged, classics, the Readers Library, which pre-dated Penguins by over a decade. What is more, Readers Library editions were hardback and turned out to be durable. My copy of *Three Men in a Boat* survives in its entirety, albeit battered, after 65 years.

Of the four Lincoln cinemas only the Grand — lately renamed from a somewhat mundane Electric — and the aforementioned Picture House were on High Street. The Grand, on the far side of the Stonebow, stood where it ended steeply, tapering like a pencil point before merging into streets that climbed towards the cathedral. The Corn Exchange cinema, a vast barn of a building, was but a few steps off High Street, however. It was on Cornhill, a square whose short skirting roads led to the market and its environs. This area seethed with vociferous life on Saturday nights, a life smacking of beer, fish and chips and earthy brushes with giggling girls, expansive in secure knowledge of Sunday morning's lay in. The Central in Silver Street completed the quartet, a cinema destined to be gutted by fire and re-built in the 'Thirties as a typically plush inter-war theatre complete with mighty Wurlitzer and the ornate decor.

Two live theatres also competed for pleasure seekers' money. The Theatre Royal, within hailing distance of the Grand Cinema, where straight plays, musical comedies and Christmas pantomimes were staged, and the Palace on Newland, a variety theatre. When talking pictures arrived the Palace changed to a cinema calling itself The Plaza.

No cinema or theatre, though, could compete in our estimation with Sincil Bank, home of Lincoln City Football Club. The Imps, as the club has always been known, naturally claimed our support as the nearest Football League outpost even though modestly in Division Three, and even if we had affections for leading sides: M, for instance, for Manchester United (originally because of Manchester family connection), and my own illogical attachment to Spurs. (Both allegiances have proved life-long). But Sincil Bank was almost local and, as a rare treat, attainable.

If in the Stonebow vicinity half an hour or so before kick-off time you might have noticed men and youths moving down High Street. They were not time killing strollers but moved purposefully. By the time the first level crossing was reached the purposeful composed nearly all the pedestrians, a cloth capped, artisan, fag-in-mouth throng. The level crossings left behind, a substantial railway bridge ahead spanning High Street heralded the turn off. (At home you could never dodge rivers; in Lincoln railways seemed unavoidable). The turn off, Sewell's Walk, had a fenced drain at one side and a line of red brick terraced houses on the other. At the street end a foot bridge led to similar houses and to their right just under another railway bridge the ground's most used entrance invitingly lay, turnstiles clicking turgidly like unwilling castanets.

At that time the inside appointments were far from palatial. The old St. Andrew's stand, against the pleasing backcloth of an ascending South Common, had a pronounced rickety look. Its roof line seemed uneven, this perhaps accentuated visually by being painted in black and white vertical stripes. Odd this — black and white stripes was the strip of arch rivals Grimsby Town! In one corner a hut served as the teams' dressing rooms, its smoking chimney indicating players' bath water had not been forgotten. The enclosure slopes, opposite the stand where we usually went, had far more banked earth and cinders than formal terracing.

The playing pitch itself, however, was magnificent, a stretch of turf that balded only in goal areas and there only late in an eight-month season. It deserved its acknowledged bracketing with Bury's Gigg Lane as the best in the whole of the Football League. In the late 'Twenties some colourful City players performed on this lush carpet. Billy Dinsdale for one, a strapping 13-stone centre-forward. "Give it to Dinny!", the crowd would chant. If the ball did reach him he often obliged with a thundering shot. Lumbering he might be but never dull. A local boy, Harold Andrews, then starting a noteworthy career, also scored frequently. A darting, quicksilver performer, too young and promising for a modest club to hold indefinitely. And at full-back Albert Worthy played: fair and squat, head titled slightly to one side above a thick neck, thighs like young oaks. Albert had a mule's kick, tackled like a tank and oozed aggression in spite of the little smile hovering round his lips.

On the high railway embankment at one end goods trains would chug past the ground at a crawl, their drivers and firemen apparently football fans too. And on the horizon beyond the embankment the mighty cathedral seemed to float as in a mirage, dominating everything in the city.

With their liking for shortening words people often referred to Skegness as Skeg. Or, alternatively, retained two syllables and called it Skeggy. These substitutes, besides being idiomatic, masked an affection for the County's most popular seaside resort. But this affection did not blind some to what they considered drawbacks. "It's Nottingham (or Derby, or Leicester) by the sea", they said, intimating that Midlands city slickers were not really our kind, that their fast ways would contaminate honest Lincolnshire virtue. Then, by the late 'Twenties, mounting summer weekend traffic brought hazards in addition to a passing show for gawpers. Cars and motor-bikes flailed through our town's twisting streets on summer Saturdays, using roads narrowed in the centre by market stalls. And — adding insult to unjury — drivers and passengers rarely stopped to spend any money.

Still, the young minded neither traffic nor junketing Midlanders: Skegness was there to be enjoyed. Enjoyed, too, in the years before the motor bus era, even though getting there entailed a daunting railway journey (and this despite being but twenty miles away). Ideas of extending our railway line north and east had foundered, so it is recorded, on lack of capital. (There were also twin difficulties of Wold terrain and a sparse population, I should have thought). So by rail we had to go, first to the inevitable Woodhall Junction — which actually took us further away — then catch a connection to Firsby, another junction, where trains had to be changed again for the final stage.

Buses altered all this. They made the journey in under one and a half hours (although it seemed longer to some allergic to fumes emitted by those innovative vehicles). Before hourly services made them unnecessary, there were excursions, especially during school summer holidays. Seats would be booked in good time and early on the great morning a massive cutting of sandwiches took pace ("Much better than the stuff you get in cafés") and carefully stowed, grease-proof paper wrapped, in Grandma's waterproof shopping bag. Weather portents coloured grown-ups' conversation. ("It won't rain today —there's too much wind" or perhaps "There's thunder about, Doug had better tek his mac"). More entertainingly a grown-up might reminisce "D'you remember Mr. and Mrs. Pridmore paddlin' last year?" And the vision of the Pridmores sampling the North Sea rose as unbidden as a hiccup. He, tall and thin, showing long underpants rolled to mid-calf (adults apparently felt cold even in summer then); she, short and fat, decorously holding her skirt but nevertheless revealing vast kneelength drawers. "The long and the short of it" Mrs. Spenloe had remarked, not very wittily. Everybody laughed, but not maliciously, because we all loved the Pridmores.

Our family never took any chances with excursion times. We unfailingly arrived early at the point of departure as if the advertised time was a hoax. "We don't like rushin'," explained the grown-ups, which although true, masked another reason — missing a bus was considered highly irresponsible. Until roughly halfway to Skegness, the bus had to chug up and down Wold hills. From the highest summits one hoped to discern a blue smudge due east and be the first to exclaim "Look Mam, there's the sea!". After the hills the terrain changed dramatically as we entered the Marshes, that wide, almost hedgeless expanse, flat as Fen country. Then, with Burgh-le-Marsh and its dominating church and six-sail windmill behind us, only the final lap remained. Soon the outer rim of Skegness could be descried, an ever expanding growth of new houses and bungalows. This growth surprised no child because nobody in his or her right mind would or could refuse to live at the seaside! But you did not *really* arrive at Skegness until, with new development behind us, our bus made an abrupt, near 90-degree swing into the long straight of Roman Bank. Another half-mile and we were bumping down a side road to the bus depot. "We leave from here at half-past seven," the driver would announce with the satisfied air of a man who had accomplished a safe delivery to a far destination. Which I suppose, by the yardstick of those days, he had.

On leaving the bus we re-emerged at the busy end of Roman Bank. People would be milling in and out of the railway station. (The thought occurred: "Fancy *leaving* Skeggy at 11 o'clock on a bright August morning!") The stone lion outside the Lion Hotel opposite invariably had a child astride. It stood just the right height and its back, smooth as a river-washed pebble, had worn positively concave.

At right angles to Roman Bank ran Lumley Road, vital inasmuch as it led directly to the sea. Even if it had been a mud tack, Lumley Road would still have seemed magical. As it was, with shops, cafés, thronged pavements and open landaus pulled by clip-clopping horses, it held the enchantment of a special gateway. Some shops had forecourts under glass canopies, there the better to display seaside paraphernalia — buckets and spades and bathing costumes and the rest. ("Did you see the price?", a scandalised Grandma would always ask Mother — she had a nose for prices rivalling that of a wine connoisseur for bouquet). Post-cards, in vertical array in their rotating racks, were the items which enticed passers-by to dally on shop forecourts. As ever, there were two types: the glossy scenic, showing beach, pier, Clocktower, pleasure grounds —prim and respectable as a parish magazine; and the bawdy. This other, the Donald McGill variety, vividly coloured stock characters, double entendre captions and all, drew a continuous stream of grinning (mostly middle-aged) men, sometimes with tut-tutting, sometimes equally appreciative, wives. If a book on working-class bawdy in the twentieth century is ever written, the McGill post-card will provide a main and indispensable source. Their skinny undersized husbands and huge domineering wives, startled clerics and amiable drunks, nubile damsels and lecherous swains, were and are as inseparable from an English seaside holiday as the kids' sand castles.

The four-faced Clocktower, at the street's end, is Skegness's best known landmark, a tall isolated monolith, standing at crossroads formed by Promenade and Pullover, the latter Lumley Road's continuation to the sea. For one excited child it was much more than an outside timepiece. As you made your way up Lumley Road, the Clocktower stood starkly fronting sky and sea, a sea whose wash could be imagined if not heard, and anticipation welled up strongly as on a Christmas Eve.

One was never disappointed. The sands, like many on the East Coast were largely free of pebbles and stretched golden as honey. Children in scores dug channels, made mud pies and sand castles, paddled, bathed, sucked rock, rode donkeys, bought and consumed ice cream. They swam, splashed, ran, shrieked, shouted, played beach cricket and football and only occasionally cried. One could hardly wait to pull off shoes and stockings and go to the water's edge, first standing to let expiring waves swirl warmly around my ankles. Then advance, half remembering grown-ups' warning "Don't go in too far", thinking to go just to where waves hit legs below rolled-up shorts and always judging wrongly. You knew then that, on returning, wet rolled-up trouser must not contact dry sand otherwise thighs would subsequently feel as if encased in emery cloth. A small price, though, to pay for such bliss.

Soon, too soon, came authority's call to return. It was time to have lunch and so be ready in good time to attend Clements' show. The grown-ups would have taken deck chairs near to a beach establishment that sold pots of tea and jugs of hot water and did not object to customers bringing their own sandwiches. The establishment also provided for customers wishing to eat indoors: there were long tables and forms standing on planks, the planks all but obscured by sand blown in and added to by the clientele. Clements' concert party, renowned throughout the East Midlands, gave afternoon performances on their beach stage and played in the evening at the Arcadia Theatre in Drummond Road. Attendance at an afternoon show was the high spot of my family grown-ups' outing. They were not alone. The deck chairs fronting the stage always seemed filled, overlooking Promenade railings always crowded. The stage was bare except for piano and backcloth. All the performers were competent and no doubt received a 'lift' from full houses and sure knowledge of being known and liked. Male members wandered at times among the audience armed with collecting boxes, immaculate in white flannels, brass-buttoned navy blue blazers and straw boaters, living versions of the still-extant seaside knut. Womenfolk thought them marvellous, radiating for them a glamour comparable to that of, say, the next decade's dance band vocalists.

Tangible momentoes of a visit to Clements' were the photographs taken of the audience and obtainable before we left for home. Several survive and one of them, judging from ladies' hats and my size (standing and yet not tall enough to obscure the view of people immediately behind) the time must have been around 1920. The audience that day — as on similar occasions — was largely composed of women. The war, so recently ended, silently revealed its aftermath in the imbalance of the sexes.

Like Skegness, Cleethorpes also had its detractors. "It's not on the sea at all, it's on the owry owd river!" and "There's too many trippers" were common jibes. On the sea or not, you certainly got the full seaside atmosphere. Especially when advancing to the lapping water's edge, bare feet delighting in the feel of warm wet rippled sand that, for me, was synonymous with Cleethorpes. And on the horizon distant Spurn Head and its lighthouse was a change from the unvarying meeting of sky and sea at other resorts. As for trippers, to a sociable seven-year-old, the more the merrier.

Anyway, I loved the place. Ross Castle, that ivy clad 'folly' on the Prom where you could chase up the winding approach path and not suffer the vertigo felt at, say, Tattershall Castle; a Prom that boasted a railway station that in turn boasted a clocktower; clanging open-topped trams to Grimsby — there were so many delights. My affection transcended that felt for Skeggy, where a tendency to be bilious reached a nadir when spectacularly sick in the aisle of the Arcadia Theatre. ("The air is too strong for him," knowing adults opined, apparently not unblinkered admirers of the bracing ozone at Skegness). We spent a whole week at Cleethorpes in 1921 and again in '22, staying in congenial digs where the host — a then rarity, a car owner — sometimes motored us to Waltham and other points south. Although motor jaunts would normally have been greatly appreciated, it seemed a pity to cut into beach time. Ploughed fields could be seen at will at home!

The smaller twin resorts, Mablethorpe and Sutton-on-Sea, never approached the liveliness of Cleethorpes and Skegness. Nor did they need to, sands gloriously golden and stretching for miles, overlooked by dunes where the sea did not reach and you sank ankle-deep into fine sand through sprouting marram grass and sea holly.

At all these places and coast villages you might see horses pulling high two-wheeled carts along beaches close to the sea. These were shrimp and cockle carts trailing their nets. The fishermen, much admired and versed in tide and weather lore, were also experts on samphire, a sea plant found in marshy land adjoining parts of the Lincolnshire and Norfolk coasts. Locals knew, and know, it as 'samfer'. Samphire is actually glasswort or, grandly 'herbs de St. Pierre'. It makes a fine pickle, crisp and tangy to the palate, as becomes an iodine-containing plant. Various recipes appear in local publications from time to time, usually in the gathering season, August and September. A typical recipe is to wash, boil in salted water for 25 minutes and serve with butter. Like asparagus, it is then eaten in the fingers.

ELEVEN : STILL WILLINGLY TO SCHOOL

It stood back from the road behind a private garden as if bashful of its comparative newness when neighbouring buildings were so obviously old. Now in the mid-1920s, red bricks of 1909 origin had scarcely weathered. Tall iron entrance gates hung from pillars topped by stone orbs. Both pillars bore inscriptions cut into stonework facing the road: GRAMMAR SCHOOL on the left, FOR BOYS AND GIRLS on the right. A short drive between a high wooden garden fence and the Reindeer Inn's ancient brick boundary wall led you there.

Each term-time morning town pupils streamed in from one direction, out of town pupils mostly from the other. The latter, largely in a single disgorgement from the railway station a mere two hundred yards away. One romantic arrived on horseback, conveniently stabling his steed at the Reindeer. The drive would be thronged for a brief spell. Thereafter, with the first clanging bell and the School in session, it remained quite empty and out of bounds to pupils until lunch time. Empty, that is, except on dry summer days when during morning break (no 'playtime' appellation here!) three youngish masters briskly trod the drive. Up-down, up-down they went, smoking convivial cigarettes, any breeze billowing out their black gowns. What did they talk about, this trio of earnest academics? The human condition — schoolmasters' salaries — Form 3B's impossible obtuseness — the foibles of the Lincolnshire young? Perhaps all these and many more.

The School had a long history. Letters patent granted by Queen Elizabeth I in 1571 were thought to re-found an institution going back two and a half centuries earlier. Longevity went hand in hand with many vicissitudes, some still green in the memories of former pupils. Before moving to these new quarters the School had functioned in an ancient building grotesquely inadequate even by spartan Victorian standards. The number of boys enrolled shrunk to the point that, in 1902, a hitherto resisted idea of taking in girl pupils was implemented. (Co-educational grammar schools similarly came about elsewhere in Lincolnshire at the time). The staff side quickly established itself quantitively as regards both teachers and pupils and, by the time of this account, secondary education locally was no more novel than the sight of a motor car.

But at the outset the change must have seemed revolutionary to masters and boys. Feminine presence inevitably brings a softening ambiance, sometimes obvious, sometimes subtly elusive. The mere fact masters and mistresses addressed girls by christian and us by surname created a feeling — no doubt unwarranted — that erring (scholastically speaking) girls were let down rather more easily, with no corresponding treatment from mistresses to us. Such male chauvinistic feelings apart, a straw poll would probably have produced a consensus that girls were good to have around. Unlike us, who had no stipulated dress except the regulation cap, girls strictly adhered to uniform with a single seasonal variance — a straw hat in summer replaced the close fitting, dome shaped headgear worn in other terms. Otherwise navy gym slips, white blouses, ties in School colours and long black stockings obtained all year through. Those black stockings that, apparently from faulty suspension, so often appeared to require adjustment! Hands placed on both sides of the leg above the knee; and the sliding, hitching, upward motion, first one leg and then the other. A delightfully feminine action somehow changing notions about girls, and one to be witnessed without appearing to do so.

The width of the main building concealed the School's extent, which culminated in a five acre playing field. This field, gently undulating and shaped like an upturned letter L, had two differing faces. In football and hockey playing terms, the far soccer pitches had old goalposts tilting at strange angles, mute symbols of inter-war making-do. Though privileged with decent goalposts, the main soccer pitch suffered from being bounded on two sides by ditches. The ball would inevitably find its way into both and gradually attain a weight that made a mistimed header leave one feeling as if concussed and making propulsion hard work even with the hefty boots then worn.

Summer naturally presented a more benign face. Gone the rickety goalposts, a neatly cut cricket square dominating that region. Tennis courts (by reluctant dispensation available to boys on Friday evenings only) emerged from eight months of lying fallow. It was pleasant on warm sunny days to laze on soft grass under an old ash tree's ample branches before the bell tolled for afternoon lessons. Thoughts came and went languid as any white wisps of cloud drifting above. The future stretched to infinity, untold delights lay ahead although reaching that old groundsman's age was quite inconceivable. He pottered stiff jointedly in the distance, thin and gnarled, hair and moustache snowy white. If scything on the outfield he resembled Old Father Time in modern garb. Sometimes in my reverie he took on a vaguely symbolic quality in which Marvell's line on Time's winged chariot figured. And ever so slightly for a brief moment spirits were blighted, for you knew that certainly you must grow old too.

The mid-morning release from lessons may have been entitled 'playtime' at elementary school and 'break' at the Grammar, but they had one thing in common: a ball game played whether or no it was the football season. However, whereas the Wesleyan School game was haphazard, that at the Grammar School had regard to which goal any individual defended or attacked. It depended on his House. When a pupil started at the School he or she was allocated to one of two Houses, Stanhope or Clinton, and remained in that House until leaving for university or paid employment. In practice the dichotomy evinced itself officially in sport — House matches at cricket, football or hockey, and athletics when separate boys' and girls' House cups were competed for on Sports Day and awarded on the basis of the day's results.

The break ball game was, of course, quite unofficial, a kickabout of few rules where rugger scores like 15-10 occurred. Traditionally Clinton defended the 'goal' nearest to the main building, i.e. the space between the corner of that edifice and tall boundary fence separating playground from a bus repair depot.

The Stanhope goal, equally traditional, the space between two stanchions of the Shed, had considerably less width. This seemed rather unfair but, as the short playground had an irregular shape, no other arrangement was feasible. Everyone excepting acknowledged goalkeepers observed the rule of not handling the small rubber or tennis ball invariably used. And there were bold spirits to retrieve it from the bus depot yard when occasion demanded. Notionally forbidden, tackling the boundary fence had its own technique: a running jump so that a foot found the middle horizontal cross-member at the same time as your hands grasped the fence top, then a quick vault over.

First acquaintance with these House clashes proved something of an eye-opener, seeing long trousered youths of 16 and 17 so disporting themselves. In the town they had appeared so lordly and aloof, and for them to take part in these contests seemed out of character. Nonetheless their control of the small ball, tapping and feinting and keeping trajectory low, earned one's envious admiration. End to end the ball sped, the high School windows a silent inducement for it to be kept low, the grazing reality of hard asphalt demanding balance. Small wonder after this that the First XI showed such mastery with a large football.

To most the games were merely a diverting means of expending energy and pleasurably filling in time at breaks or before afternoon lessons. Exceptions were two friends, both in the upper School. One, tall and leggy, jinked and flitted in sinuous dribbles for the Stanhope cause with a concentration worthy of a less transient endeavour. The other, squat and dour, defended the Clinton goal, unsmiling and steadfast. A Lincolnshire Horatius defending his bridge.

Between the main building and playing field were sited the School's other amenities. Immediately behind the main building were parallel boys' and girls' playgrounds, divided by a high close-boarded fence and terminatd with a wall that provided the base for a hipped roof on stanchions which gave cover in wet breaks and was known as the Shed. This wall's other side served as a back for the cycle shed, a simple corrugated-iron awning protecting the cycle racks. At right angles to the cycle shed stood a long low building that dated from 1913. It contained two non-communicating halves — a girls' domestic science room and boys' carpentry workshop, dubbed Cookery and Woodwork respectively. And, on the other side of the final strip before the playing field was reached, stood The Hut.

The Hut. Not, you will note, 'a hut' but The Hut, always in speech capital letters implied. Because the words, for those whose School careers coincided with The Hut's existence, conjure up a clear recollection of hollow sounding plank floors, old desks whose lids were immovable and an atmosphere always a little dust-laden.

In the early 1920s the School faced a dilemma: accommodation too small to take increased numbers in an era of belt-tightening retrenchment. Its solution was to purchase, dismantle and re-erect a wooden Army barrack room and convert it into three formrooms. Thus The Hut came into being to house, among others, in its shabby interior a dozen or more annual intakes of new Grammarians until the mid-1930s brought a new permanent building.

Each September the intake composed the new bottom form, 3B; thirty or so initially subdued young mortals equally divided between the sexes. Dispositions in the usual, apparently immutable, mode were made — facing the blackboard, girls' desk columns on the left, boys' on the right. New subjects came to plague us. French, for instance, where the master in this first year inculcated the language aided by large pictures and a boy-taming expedient. The pictures, four in number depicting the seasons, were draped over the blackboard and pupils went out singly to point out objects when commanded in French by the master. (A worrying business in our year for a boy who would advance nervously to the picture absent-mindedly scratching his behind, thus acquiring for a time the nickname Trousers). The boy-taming expedient consisted of the master taking a tuft of boy's hair a couple of inches above his ear and twisting it. As an aid to learning (and discipline) it proved effective.

The Hut's separateness conferred an advantage. When a lesson ended our instructor left and the one for the next had to make his or her way from the main building. So several minutes respite could be devoted to letting off pent-up feelings and a rare racket ensued. A fairly circumspect buzz of talk from girls, a louder, more spasmodic and raucous volume from the boys. More privately, a comparing of notes between the academically ambitious, the arrangement of an after-school tryst between friends.

Dictionaries give several meanings to the word 'Olympian' when not specifically relating to Greek gods and dwellers upon Mount Olympus. They include a person very important or stately, godlike and someone of superhuman calmness and detachment. Though the word was not in one's vocabulary at the age of twelve, there were encounters with a living Olympian. Doubtless our Headmaster did not possess all the listed qualities but stateliness and detachment certainly, and frequently 'godlike' did not seem all that inappropriate. Over six feet tall, ramrod straight, grizzled thinning hair and moustache always in the same condition of trimmed neatness, he appeared to radiate omnipotence. By the mid-1920s he had held the Headmastership some two decades, eventually to retire on the completion of a quarter of a century, full of years and to most still an enigma

Advancing years had not noticeably mellowed a character naturally austere. Pronouncements of wrong-doing before the assembled School at the conclusion of morning prayers had the effect of Jehovian anger: terrible to contemplate. (Apparently the depth of wrong-doing was to be seen talking to a girl in the town). And when in Form 3A the Headmaster for some reason took over Maths periods, it at first resembled being forced into the ambit of a deity — frightening. He had great belief in constantly checking whether a point had sunk in and woe betide the unfortunate whose hand failed to go up. We quickly learned it better to put up one's hand whether knowing the answer or not on the sporting odds of 30-1 on not being asked. The ruse worked most times, of course, and when it did not a muffed answer or no answer at all might, if lucky, merely provoke a cutting "Hypocrite!" But when unlucky he would pause, remove his spectacles, wither one with a look that curled the stomach and give vent to righteous anger.

The Head's real subject was History and here, amid the tension and evasive action to steer clear of trouble, emerged delight. (There is but one solitary recollection of his losing temper during a History period; when nobody could name Antwerp's river. The whole Form was sentenced to write a hundred lines, "Antwerp stands on the River Scheldt"). It happened that even those antipathetic to the subject started to progress and marks at end-of-term exams went up accordingly. His method involved the unexpected divergence. You would never know where a lesson would lead. An investigation into Marlborough's campaigns branched off, among many other unrelated topics, into the poetry of Alfred Noyes (because the Head found the surname amusing); the story of a visitor to the Zoo seeing a cage labelled "Dangerous" and thinking it to be the name of occupants' species (pronounced Dangeroos); during the 1928 Salvation Army leadership crisis, a brilliant impromptu sketch of that worthy body's history; a reasoned discourse on why we should tackle for pleasure the novels of Stanley Weyman, and one listener at least found the recommendation very worthwhile.

A complex personality, sometimes showing a sudden flash of awareness of one's existence outside the form room. A day, for instance, when looming up during break saying "You have shot up lately", thereupon escorting me indoors to personally ascertain my height. Sometimes sardonically — "So you like playing with a soft ball", on noting my liking for Friday evening tennis. His involvement in affairs outside School seemed non-existent, but he was a regular cinema-goer.

Long afterwards came the notion that at bottom he was a shy man.

As with countless comparable institutions, the outside world impinged on the School twice a year: on Speech and Sports Days. Ours were tidily separated by six months; Speech Days in December, Sports Days in June. The School did not then possess an actual assembly hall, a deprivation to be belatedly remedied in 1937, and the cinema housed our Speech Day throng. It was an odd coupling, a formal and staid School occasion held in the local temple of waking-dream fantasy.

Masters and mistresses were seated on stage, gowns now embellished by variously coloured and furred hoods draping throat and shoulders, and wearing mortar-boards. A table piled with prize books stood in the centre, behind which sat the Headmaster and the bigwig who would present them. The buzz of talk as the hall filled with parents and pupils, low pitched but unremitting as a well maintained turbine, ceased instantly when the Head rose. He would review the School year: so many university scholarships won, so many school certificate and matriculation passes gained, a good record in pinchpenny times from accommodation too small, hopes for the future — an even larger number of exam successes, for new buildings to ease the space problem. The Head's speech hardly seemed to vary from one year to the next. Nor did the bigwig's, even though a fresh one pontificated every time. He or she would exhort us to work hard, be respectful of authority, play the game. He or she could tell us some homilies from his or her own schooldays (and proceeded to do so at length) illustrating the truths contained in the initial exhortations. He or she thereupon sat down to perfunctory clapping. The prizes were distributed and we poured out into the December murk feeling somewhat drained but revived rapidly on remembering Christmas was but two or three weeks away.

Much the same audience, of course, attended Sports Day, Parents and relations sat on a crescent of chairs placed halfway round the circular laned running-track which had been carefully marked out the previous day. That morning the chairs had been delivered with the assistance of selected School huskies piled high on a horse-drawn dray. Tomorrow they would be returned by the same method to their home, the former Grammar School building now serving as a church hall.

Fine weather always seemed to bless Sports Days. June afternoons breezy enough to stir concentrated leafage on tree and hedgerow, sunny enough to have enticed ladies into bright summery dresses. The Games Master, armed with a megaphone, conducted proceedings with practised aplomb, aided by other masters and a couple of fathers whose one-time athletic renown was still green locally. The Games Mistress efficiently dovetailed her girls' events into the programme. At a distance from track and spectators, the Town Band went through its repertoire unhurriedly. Behind the crescent of chairs the Headmaster hovered.

Birds sang, apparently undisturbed, the scene was as English as a maypole dance, as wholesome as fresh fruit. God was in his heaven, the Great War a decade behind us. There could not possibly be another war in the foreseeable future, could there?

For no reason other than alliteration — which could have been accidental —everybody called her Sally. And, for an obvious reason, everybody looked forward to her classes or, at the very least, had no anticipatory qualms. An almost carnival air pervaded when one instructor left and English was down as the next period. In The Hut, inter-lesson hubbubs only partially abated on her entry. "You can always play up old Sal," they said or "Sally lets you get away with it".

Actually the nickname 'Sally' denoted Miss M. L. Sinclair, MA (Honours in English), Edinburgh University; Trained Certificated Teacher. She did not enter a form room in the accepted meaning of entering so much as sail in, black gown billowing, plump body slightly tilted forward, red cheeked, dark bobbed hair just starting to grey and unfailingly smiling to reveal white even teeth.

Apparently no book dating from later than 1850 met school certificate requirements, no equivalent of *Lord of the Flies* or *To Kill a Mockingbird* (which later examinees studied) could be sanctioned. The thought occurs that Sally dilating, say, on *A High Wind in Jamaica* and *The Good Companions* would have been illuminating. Even if our occasional attempts to divert her by making outrageous comparisions (e.g. the superiority of Edgar Wallace and Sapper over the authors we 'suffered') were anything to go by. A legitimate occasion for comparison came at the time of our Edgar Wallace phase just before our school certificate year. Robert Bridges had recently died thus rendering the post of Poet Laureate vacant. Who, enquired Sally, should be awarded the crown? The form, practically unanimously, plumped for Rudyard Kipling. Sally at

The South Front.

A vintage season when every match was won. Back row: (left to right) K. C. F. Belton, the author, G. I. Smith, F. E. Kemp, T. W. Belton, J. H. Warner; front row: A. G. Blackburn, F. N. Buttery, J. Vickers, C. Warner, F. W. Belton. The XI was made up of 4 future schoolmasters, a university lecturer, 2 civil servants, a company managing director, a policeman and 2 Services regulars, one in the Army and the other in the RAF. There were two sets of brothers: Ken and Freddie Belton (Tom was not related) and Jim and Cyril Warner. Sadly, both Beltons and Jim Warner lost their lives flying with the wartime RAF. At the time this caption was composed (February 1990) it is thought there are 5 survivors. The line-up shows the School's wide catchment area – besides 6 'locals' there were 3 from Congingsby, 1 from Bardney and 1 from Moorhouses.

once launched into a consummately argued discourse on the why and wherefores of his not getting the appointment, and accurately forecasting that John Masefield would.

Sally loved literature and had the rare gift of passing on that love to her unruly assemblies. Over the years we tackled Scott's prose (*Ivanhoe*) and blank verse, *Lady of the Lake* and *Marmion*, Dickens (chiefly *David Copperfield*) and Shakespeare. All were revealed as many-faceted as a cut diamond. The rich Shakespearean language soaked in, Dickens's multitudinous characters emerged in the round, Scott's daunting industry displayed. And Sally was no fool. She unerringly picked on M to read out the bawdier Shakespeare lines, M being the sole guaranteed poker-face in a form of aware adolescents.

Sally married late and died comparatively young. Her gentle lilting Scots voice remains fresh in memory after sixty years. She implanted a love of books for so many, I hope she knew.

A 'Long Morning' meant an extra period tacked on to morning school in order that the afternoon period finished at 2.45. Long mornings were infrequent in Christmas and Easter terms, occurring only when the 1st XI had a home match. Short winter afternoons postponed our touch-line support until part of the first half was over. So, as a 3B minnow in The Hut, seeing the 1st XI troop by gave one a thrill. Impressive in their red and blue vertically striped jerseys and asphalt-rasping studded boots, these mid- and late-teen demigods seemed living embodiments of sporting attainment. It was unlikely one could reach the eminence of a place in the XI eventually; still one could dream ...

Long mornings prevailed throughout the Summer term when cricket and swimming came into their own. The field echoed with the sound of bat striking leather; a sound, by the way, seldom obliterated by shouting. The Head liked to drift from game to game; a tall, near expressionless, bowler hatted figure whose mere presence strangled any stridency. The main cricket square was cosseted like a cherished child. The groundsman fussed around it and teams of juniors, under an unrelenting senior, were detailed to pull the big roller up and down the square's length after school hours. We enlivened the chore with song, principally *The Volga Boatman* with 'Volga' inevitably changed to 'Vulgar'.

The School took over the public swimming baths four afternoons each week during the Summer term: Mondays and Fridays for girls, Tuesdays and Thursdays for boys. (Wednesdays were sacrosanct for workers released from their labours by half-day closing). The baths were not far distant — a curving quarter-mile skirting the station yard to where the two rivers joined and then across a wooden foot-bridge (in all town journeys an unavoidable bridge to cross!) The baths lay end-on to the now united river, a squat black rectangle of high wooden walls, in part barbed-wire topped, which a stranger would have found difficult to identify but for the sound of splashing and laughter. This sombre exterior belied the cheerful scene within. And even cubicle ceilings danced a welcome, an open space above door lintels allowing reflections of the pool's constantly disturbed water. A happy presage this to the delicious pleasure of immersion on a hot day, water refreshing one's body totally.

The School had devised an excellent method for creating swimmers. A boy who could swim instructed a non-swimmer until he too could swim unaided. As one's instructor was invariably older and bigger, duckings and other minor tortures were liable to reward incompetence. Most novices learned remarkably quickly.

In aquatic sport, no boy could compare with Walley, whose rotund frame assumed an assured gace in water absent out of it. In the crawl his glistening arms skimmed rhythmically as a metronome. From high and low springboards he dived like an inspired salmon, leaping high, twisting forwards or backwards — the full repertoire of a naturally gifted water sprite. A subsequent swimming half-Blue at Oxford seemed but natural justice.

He stood out from the ruck of School hearties like a small, elegant courtier amid peasantry. Fine boned, golden hair longish by 'Twenties standards and swept across his forehead, attire always faultless, slacks' crease knife-edged. Such was John Stanley Richardson, perhaps the most brilliant scholar in the School's history, certainly in living memory.

By this time Richy (as we call called him), in the Sixth Form and a prefect, had the assurance of acceptance and acclaim. But how did he fare, one wonders, on entering the School in 1921, a free-placer in his tenth year and, presumably even then, an exquisite? He appeared to be exempt from games, a law unto himself. His presence on the field was for strolling purposes only, in the company of George K, his sole intimate who played, in a manner of speaking, Dr. Watson to Richy's Sherlock Holmes. Their figures contrasted greatly. Richy's slender as a girl's, George's just as short but bulky; Richy fair and clear skinned, George dark and, like many of us, inclined to teen spottiness.

Generally boys viewed Richy with a kind of puzzled awe, rather as an ordinary family might on spawning a prodigy. There could be no sharing of sporting preoccupations either in active playing or in following the deeds of contemporary athletic heroes, for he occupied a different plane. Sometimes on finding yourself alone with him you might try a tentative "Richy, have you read (say) H. G. Wells?" He always had and, perfectly courteous, flash a toothy smile and add a few words on Wells's differing roles as comic novelist and scientific guru. Not condescending exactly but plainly it was no parley between equals either. He doubtless thought us a set of well meaning bumblers, at best pleasantly tolerable. If he did expand conversationally the words gushed out as a public proclamation rather than a remark for the faithful George's ear alone. "I think I prefer Miss Hare to the rest of our appointed instructors," he might loudly trill. (Miss Hare, the senior mistress, whose subjects were Latin and Divinity). Or, book in hand, with splendid (and, not unlikely, justified) arrogance, "I think this translation is wrong."

He left for Cambridge to be elected Jebb Student in European History and Literature. He published some well-praised lyric verse, lectured in America, met the great and famous and was killed in a London air-raid in 1941. He was 29.

He whom the gods favour dies young.

I suppose every school has its cavalier character. That is, a vaguely raffish boy

145

largely impervious to, and holding scant respect for, authority. Clever enough to steer clear of real troble, admired by younger boys, flattered by hangers-on, he goes his own unpredictable way. Staid souls, often envious of his quicksilver appeal, may demur but are not above relishing his latest exploit.

Such a one was Clicker, by 1928 the School's undisputed champion noncomformist. Clicker: seldom wearer of the supposedly always-worn School cap, wearer of trousers with bottoms reckoned prodigiously wide even in that era of Oxford bags, of the consistently bantering approach, inveterate first teller of the latest risqué story. Clicker: smoker of cigarettes on School premises, midday thumper-out of dance tunes on the sacred School piano; once caught by a scandalised music master midway through a jazzed up rendition of *Sonny Boy*, Clicker just smiled winningly and escaped with a caution.

His home was some miles away so he held court at lunch time. Perched on the cloakroom wash basins, flanked by henchmen, his quipping was scarcely checked by a steady consumption of sandwiches and thermos flask tea. Nobody ever bested Clicker in argument. His nimble wit soon swamped anyone foolhardy enough to try and his henchman — he never appeared to be solitary — always added their weight to his cause.

His sporting displays were absolutely in parallel. As the 1st XI's outside-left he sped down the wing like a deer with a somewhat high-kneed lope, occasionally scoring brilliant individual goals but more often shooting wide. As the opposing wing-half in house matches, I could testify to the difficulties of marking him. Tackles tended to be bruising affairs but had to be endured because, once past, it was all but impossible to catch him. At cricket he believed in either scoring or getting out. No playing oneself in for Clicker, his limited patience did not permit so prosaic an approach.

Equally in character, his reputation as a lady killer. At School girls eyed Clicker with the kind of wary approval their elder sisters might have given to a sophisticated man of the world. As so often in these cases, he had no outstanding physical attributes other than thick, naturally crinkly, hair. But he had a cool knowingness beyond his years, applying just the right amount of flattery combined with enough offhandedness to keep a girl guessing.

At the close of the Christmas term came the School Party, the sole occasion when the sexes got together socially under the School's aegis. The main building form rooms were cleared of desks, the intervening screens pushed back as at morning prayers and the floor waxed. A four-piece dance band pumped out the popular melodies of the day as we shuffled round displaying dancing skills ranging from competent to abysmal. At Clicker's last Party it was noticed he danced mostly with the School's femme fatale who enjoyed a reputation equivalent to Clicker's. Greek had indeed met (if that was the word) Greek. It was next noted the pair were no longer around and the excited tidings, from some unidentified source, went round the room "Clicker's taken her up the field!". On reflection it is hard to imagine a more uninviting sport for a romantic tryst as the playing field on a December night. Nonetheless from that night Clicker's renown, already huge, was quite unassailable.

Clicker, too, died young, a car accident the cause, following, it was said, an evening's revel. The ending, though infinitely regrettable, seemed not inappropriate, the kind of way he would go. For somehow it is impossible to imagine him growing old or even middle-aged. He is forever fixed in memory as a mocking iconoclast, but there lay life and merriment in abundance also.

"Pity we haven't a school magazine," I said one day, thinking of those delectable tit-bits in the *Magnet* when its centre pages reproduced *The Greyfriars Herald.*

"If we had, the Fifth and Sixth would hog all the space," said a cynical but realistic Blackie.

"Yes," agreed Plum, "with Richy & Co. rantin' on about Virgil."

We chortled at this, having a low opinion of Latin in general and Virgil in particular.

"Why not have a form magazine?", enquired Sugar.

The talk ceased for a moment, each turning over the idea in his mind.

"Now I know why Sally says Sugar is full of ideas", I said. (The English mistress had not long before remarked on his habit of exploring unusual avenues in homework essays).

"Good old Sugar," grinned M "Let's do it."

"Tres bien," chimed in Freddie who (perversely, we thought) loved French and was destined to specialise in the language at university.

"We don't want the lassies in on this, do we?" asked M.

"Crikey, no," said Plum, "they would write about clothes an' fashion an' Rudolph Valentino".

We were all agreed as to the desirability of not publishing feminine trivia.

Blackie asked: "What shall we call it?"

"How about *The Remove Times?*" Sugar volunteered.

We agreed the title could not be improved. We were currently members of 4B and much enjoyed the notion of being in the form equivalent to that of Billy Bunter and Harry Wharton at Greyfriars.

"He's brilliant isn't he?" said Freddie, referring to Sugar's latest suggestion, "un homme remarkable or, should I say, un garçon remarkable?"

"No more French, mon petit oiseau," M remonstrated, pulling Freddie's ear. Freddie was the youngest boy in the form, and at this time the smallest excepting for the recently-arrived Tiddler, whose family had moved to Bardney from outside the county. It was customary not to give Fredde too much latitute.

"What about illustrations?"

"Well, Duggie can do the cover," said an unrepentant Freddie. (I had a quite undeserved reputation as an artist on the strength of a flashy facility for sketching faces).

"And M can do the funnies. I'll do a sports column," Sugar followed on, who knew round holes for round pegs when he saw them. He himself was a fine all-rounder — a natural games player and strong in most academic subjects, while M's capacity for laughter had no known limits.

Blackie, Plum and Freddie said they would pen contributions and so *The Remove Times* was born.

My first cover depicted a squealing baby, to symbolise the arrival of a new publication. It had been copied from an advertisement in our *News Chronicle* with no qualms as to artistic plagiarism and without acknowledgement to the source of inspiration. O blithe innocent of 14!

Contributions were copied out by divers hands whose writing had neatness and legibility, and the magazine proved a great success on publication. Miss Sinclair expressed delight, perhaps thinking the enterprise had been sparked off by her English instruction (which maybe in a contibutory sense it had). The girls of 4B, unaware they had been deliberately excluded, tended to be admiring. Even the Headmaster expressed approval.

If memory serves, *The Remove Times* ran to three issues, the term ended and so did the magazine. The next term we were in the Remove no longer but made up the new Form 4A.

It may sound quite out of proportion, infer an ignorance of true values, a sad lack of perspective. But nothing that has happened since, and very little has equalled, the exhilaration on seeing one's name on the 1st XI team sheet for the first time. Receiving news of successfully passing professional exams, for instance, or seeing one's name on a book cover had their own thrill, yet even they did not give a greater elation.

Naturally, at 14 or 15, everything is so intense. Joys are lyrical, setbacks catastrophic. A small humiliation assumes the size of a disgrace never likely to be lived down. Conversely, an elevation such as this produced an immense glow that lasted for days. It was not unique. Forty years on M told me of a similar elation and then being cast down when an illness postponed his debut. The sight through his window on match day of a team-mate going School-wards carrying boots and playing kit held a poignancy still felt on recall.

Reasons for this apparent lack of proportion are several. The town's obsession with the game and the resultant atmosphere imbibed when growing up. Our elders' unspoken but implied certainty soccer was *the* game (remember the cricket club resumed only in 1925 after many years' dormancy). And two of our masters performed regularly and creditably in adult football.

So pulling on that red and blue jersey gave momentous pleasure. Returning to School in September after the long summer vacation was welcome simply because soccer would be played again. Even bus journeys to away matches were bearable — Froz, the skipper, and I sat together in a front seat, at the time a subdued twain to whom buses gave stomach queasiness. Behind us the rest joked and talked, the games master benignly joining in. Afterwards the match would be minutely analysed and discussed until preparations started for the next. Memories flood back: the mud and bruises, the rapture when we won (which we usually did), post-match tiredness, a feeling of being part of a team ...

It was the Headmaster's custom to patrol the main corridor. Stately as any potentate he walked slowly, hands clasped behind his back and tucked into the folds of his gown. Sometimes a mortar-board enhanced the effect but, head covered or no, his tall figure was a picture of scholarly dignity.

Bullimore had the habit of walking fairly rapidly, head down and eyes surveying a point not more than a couple of strides ahead, like an experienced soldier in India warily on the watch for snakes. Bullimore, of our form, had in early teens a weighty stockiness foretelling manhood strength.

A dire event occurred when we were in 4B. The bell had just gone for afternoon lessons and the Head emerged from his study at the end of a little passage near the boys' entrance He adopted his usual routine, walking with a measured tread, hands clasped behind, keeping to the left, so allowing a stream of boys plenty of space in which to enter the form rooms on the right.

Ours was midway along the corridor and the Headmaster had nearly reached it.

So had Bullimore.

He marched immediately behind the Headmaster, eyes as ever scanning the floor, gaining on the Head with every stride.

Those of us to the rear of Bullimore watched fascinated on realising what could happen. The tramp of many feet prevented any stage whispering to warn Bullimore, who appeared lost in thought anyway.

"This is impossible," I remember thinking, "it just can't happen."

But it did.

Bullimore 's lowered skull caught the Headmaster plumb in the small of his back, butting him in the manner of a billy-goat. The Head pitched forward but miraculously did not fall.

The world stood still.

The Head turned, his face contorted and awful in its anger. His whole being shrieked of outrage, of dignity bruised beyond bearing.

"You *idiot!*", stormed the Head, the words coming out with a breathy vehemence never heard before (nor perhaps ever again). A god had been maligned.

Poor Bullimore stood as if petrified, his normally ruddy complexion turned ashen.

We heard no more, retreating info the form room not knowing whether to laugh or be grave, but knowing we had witnessed a momentous, unbelievable happening.

Amazingly Bullimore survived. Perhaps just as amazingly, the Headmaster seemed a lot more human afterwards.

TWELVE : WITH BENEFIT OF HINDSIGHT

Writing nearly sixty years after their end, the 'Twenties take on the aspect of a vanished age, as indeed it is. The Second World War separates inter-war years in the minds of those who lived through them like a fence. And, even without this fence, technological advance and wider spread amenities make our lot in the 'Twenties appear primitive. In neighbouring villages and even on the town's periphery piped water and main drainage were a generation or more away, public electricity a decade. Gramophones that had to be cranked, cat's whisker wireless sets and silent films now seem like museum pieces.

Materially, then, there is really no comparison. From wordly goods — housing, furnishings, labour saving devices, on-tap entertainment gadgets, personal transport — to physical well being, our latter day townsman is infinitely better off. Whether he is proportionately happier, or as happy, is not so certain. Nor is his degree of contentment likely to be as high, if only because of greater expectation: our 'Twenties expectations were low or, if not low, extremely moderate.

Our earliest townsman, despite his limited means, did enjoy a significant monetary stability. For everyday items a newspaper went on costing a penny, a boys' weekly twopence, ten cigarettes sixpence, twenty eleven pence ha'penny: prices apparently immutable. This stability is confirmed by a graph published by the *Observer* in 1972. It showed a year by year values of the £ in comparison to 1914, which was taken as 100. Figures for the 1920s are:

1921	44½
1922	54½
1923	57½
1924	57
1925	57½
1926	58
1927	59½
1928	60
1929	61
1930	63½

So, after an initial, and afterwards uncharacteristic 44½ in 1921 — which followed 46½ in 1919 and 40 in 1920 — yearly figures varied only over a 9 point range for the rest of the decade.

Random reference to advertisements in the 1922 and 1920 editions in a series of football annuals reflects price stability in goods. For example:

	1922	**1930**
Football boots	9/6d — £1	16/6d
McGregor footballs	£1.7.6d.	£1.3.11d — £1.5.11d.
Raincoats	£1.10.0d.	17/7d — £1.15.0d.
High-priced macs	from £3	£2.15.0d.

150

It is stating the obvious, of course, to say an individual's attitude to an era personally lived through is conditioned, wholly or part, by his own age when the era occurred. Yet how often is this fact ignored by makers of sweeping superficial generalisations? A mature person in the 1920s — not necessarily of dyspeptic inclination — might, and often did, view the decade with distaste. A decade of wild parties and shameless short-skirted hussies and lowered standards all round, they thought. Conversely, a 'Twenties apologist would regard the relaxation of old constraints as 'A Good Thing'. A child's-eye view accorded with neither. A child sees people and environment straight and clear because he has no previous eras to make comparisons with. His self deceptions are for the most part undeveloped (and in this instance an elementary school playground provided an effective antidote for budding self deceptions). So we accepted completely the scene as it was, accepting without comment the several eccentrics still alive and flourishing. Unless, that is, an eccentric did something *especially* peculiar. As for instance the man who would not sleep in his own house in case it caught fire. The chance of his lodgings catching fire apparently did not occur to him.

The decade unfolded to increasing awareness rather like a slow moving film. The contrast between our placid surroundings and advancing technology elsewhere (e.g. in aeronautics) was marked. For the town seemed to be changeless, incapable of meaningful expansion. Lack of monetary means hardly came to mind as an explanation because we felt — wrongly — conditions had always been pretty much as they were, and always would be. So the half dozen new dwellings built during the 'Twenties assumed a distinction conferred by rarity.

Grown-ups were treated with a respect that later generations would have deemed excessive. Not just omnipotent teachers but grown-ups in the mass although teachers ranked first. That is why the Ben Shearling affair caused such a sensation. By the summer term of 1924 Ben Shearling had celebrated his fourteenth birthday and was due to leave school at the July breaking-up. He was a stocky lad, broad of shoulder and sturdy of leg, attributes that had been put to good use at right-back in the Wesleyan School's football team. One morning we in the Standard 5 desks, which occupied the bottom part of the Big Room, were suddenly aware of a particularly heated Mr. Waymouth being answered back. He was taking a combined Standards 6 and 7 in an arithmetic lesson. Then we saw Mr. Waymouth hauling a struggling Ben the length of the Big room, up the side aisle, past the war memorial and past our class to the exit door, Ben blubbering and attempting to hack Mr. Waymouth's shins as if openly arguing was not enormity enough to make the incident quite remarkable. So remarkable, in fact, my contemporaries still recall it three generations later, still awe struck at the incident's uniqueness in the climate of 1924.

A sequel nearly as earth shaking ensued that very afternoon. Ben's father stormed into the school demanding to see Mr. Waymouth. According to Mr. Shearling, an incipient boil on Ben's neck had burst during his summary removal, a calamity which made the irate parent more irate still. The two men diappeared into a corridor but we could still hear their voices. Particularly Mr. Shearling's — besides being loud his discourse was liberally peppered with

151

words later collectively referred to as four lettered. After about ten minutes Mr. Shearling departed, still grumbling and far from mollified. A sour faced though unvanquished Mr. Waymouth re-entered the Big Room, audibly snorted "What language!" and that, so far as we knew, ended the matter.

Mr. Shearling's descent on the school was most unusual for a reason other than a display of belligerence. To see an adult relative on school premises had a strange novelty. (The School Treat sports and other events which they attended were not held within school bounds). The average working class parent appeared to hold school teachers in great awe — open days' and evenings when parents met teachers to discuss their offspring's progress were well into the future.

Though the town and its environs was the only locality we children knew well, and we took things as they were and always would be, poverty at times became apparent even to our inexperienced and usually heedless selves. In, for example, the following typical elementary school exchange, which could and did happen any time:

Teacher: "Why weren't you at school yesterday?"

Child: "Please, miss, I'ed to stay at 'ome while my boots was bein' mended."

The child's reply was neither frivolous nor untrue. He or she possessed only one pair of boots and the stark choice lay between staying at home or coming to school in stocking feet. The teacher would not normally press matters further beyond suggesting the boots be repaired on a Saturday next time. Fortunately for school attendance records, those children rarely required cobblers' attention. Soles and heels were impaled with masses of sprigs that were long lasting and, incidentally, quite admirable for spark making and frosty day slides.

Out of school, tramps were still a common sight; sometimes youngish and physically powerful but mostly middle-aged, or old and worldly worn, all in the tatters that proclaimed their status. All the same, tramps could not have been as numerous as before the Great War. A 1912 newspaper report on the subject said "...the tramp nuisance is getting worse", a comment made after the justices had ruled on seven begging cases in a single week. Six of the seven tramps received a week's hard labour, the seventh, two weeks. This particular batch was not, it appears, a phenomenon. Tramps, many of them lately convicts, descended on Lincolnshire from all parts of England in those Edwardian years, the natives' innate open-handedness acting like a magnet.

A continuing, if lessening, number of vagrants in the early 1920s showed they still looked upon Lincolnshire as favourable territory. And that the natives showed customary generosity in spite of dwindling amounts to spare. Wages and salaries were falling, with the Civil Service's Geddes axe often copied elsewhere. Average farm wages in Lincolnshire fell from 40/6d in 1919 to 36/-in 1924, and farm wages were reckoned to be the bench mark by which all others could be judged.

Somewhat unfairly there existed an inclination to place two other types of intinerant very little higher than tramps. Unfair because they performed a useful service, but logical because they were strangers and strangers represented the unknown. One especially was an unknown quantity, a real foreigner possessing but a modicum of English. He was a Spaniard hawking onions which dangled from a pole balanced on his shoulder. The other travelling type was certainly native — the men who sharpened knives, scissors and shears. They trundled machines that were actually frames incorporating a grinding stone. In use a treadle-operated belt turned the stone.

How did an ordinary young couple achieve marriage in such a time of widespread depression and lack of prospects?

They did so in the same way as their forbears. Firstly, house rents were low due to a combination of the Rent Restriction Acts and the simple brute fact of low wages. (Even in 1935, when we were recovering from the depression, the average weekly wage in the town was estimated at only £2). The rent for a cottage or a small terrace house — two rooms up and two down — was accordingly but a few shillings a week. And with a population then tending to decrease, such accommodation often became available.

Like rents, furniture and other household necessities were cheap. It was a commonplace saying between the wars that one could furnish a little house for £100. Needless to say, this sum was not within the compass of all young couples. But they could at least afford some new items and, on an old relative's home being broken up, sticks of furniture were handed down as heirlooms. Three generations on from the 1920s, there must be scores of Lincolnshire homes still containing items that have been handed down several tmes, many such deserving better than a dismissive 'stick of furniture' tag. Items that are pleasing to the eye and have utility value also. Chests of drawers, for instance, massive, weighty and highly polished, able to accommodate all the bed linen and folding clothes of an average-sized family. Our house contained some pieces which were extremely old and inherited by one or other of my grandparents. For example, the dresser relegated to the back kitchen when we acquired a wireless. This generously proportioned piece included three capacious drawers and, at one end, a cupboard that was a full dresser height and depth. The cupboard, shelved at the back, easily stored all dining table equipment — table cloth, large cruet, cutlery, sugar bowl, place mats — in addition to bulky objects like an earthenware jar (holding 4lbs of sugar) and jars of preserves.

Lastly, young couples would have learned to be resourceful. As a child the girl had acquired skill in cooking and in the sewing, darning and mending of clothes. Now married, she made food spin out, never wasting a thing. The man would have the ability to improvise in heavier tasks of making their little home snug. And taking full advantage of any attached garden land, keeping a pig and a few chickens if facilities allowed.

No hint of adult 'Twenties cynicism coloured attitudes in boys' literature, attitudes exemplified in purest form in the *Boys' Own Paper*. BOP attitudes were, in fact, unchanged from those of its beginning long before the 1914 War when G. A. Henty was a contributor. They included regular recommendations to take cold baths, eat moderately and cultivate temperate habits generally. Which was not surprising for a publication having the Religious Tract Society as overseer. All this may seem slightly comic to later eyes no longer viewing matters in black and white terms. BOP fiction was also predictably mannered: foreigners either odd, funny or, if not wicked, lamentably devious. Heroes (British, of course) were paragons of courage and manliness and evidently without blemish.

But the BOP had solid virtues outweighing chauvinist imbalance. It published useful hints in making things, the welfare of pets and ridding oneself of acne. Its "Answers to Correspondents" showed good sense besides an ambience of muscular Christianity.

With all the open and hidden (though recognised) signs of hard times, school leavers tended to be realistic. Ambitions, if any, were fixed on the feasible. Ambitions, however, for most hardly entered into the matter. A town of three and a half thousand souls set in the centre of a thinly populated agricultural district at a time of depression offered little.

Each autumn a few academically inclined high fliers left for university or training college. Not in some cases, one would think, without sacrifice from moderately circumstanced parents who had no experience of advanced education themselves. Such parents' attitude to education was interesting (and continued to be as a constantly repeated country-wide phenomenon). They wanted their children to do better than they had, rightly saw educational qualification as a certain means to this end and commendably made the necessary sacrifices. But for the most part they viewed education purely in a materialistic sense: as the key to a well paid position. Understandable, of course, but surely it is more, much more, than this: a tool to enrich the recipient's life, enabling him to enter realms of interest and delight otherwise closed. Not that the least shred of reproach should attach to these parents. They saw only the concrete and knew not that a world of ideas, art and intellectual riches beyond mere utility existed.

Apart from the half dozen college bound, how were the town's several score school leavers absorbed each year? Practically without exception farmers' sons farmed, in the fullness of time inheriting the family acres or becoming masters elsewhere by marriage or gift. Similarly bakers' sons usually became bakers and naturally with other callings there was a strong tendency for boys to go into family businesses.

Of the remaining majority, shops took a proportion, particularly girls. Boys engaged as shop errand boys might be dismissed two years later. On reaching the age of sixteen, health and employment cards had to be stamped, to which cost an employer contributed. It paid the employer, therefore, to replace the sixteen-year-old with a new school leaver. Employers of newly engaged school leavers could be suspicious as well as penny pinching. One such, who had the stone floor of his office scrubbed daily, was wont to leave a shilling on the floor to test a new boy's honesty (a ruse told by one of his errand boys to the successor). After the latter had twice been tested he told his immediate superior that, if a shilling was left on the floor a third time, he would keep it. The threat was tactfully conveyed to the employer who henceforth dropped no more shillings in that boy's time. Incidentally, this employer held prominent appointments at his place of worship.

Several fortunates were taken on to learn a trade, to the justifiable satisfaction of relatives. ("Always larn a trade if y'can, y'doant want t'be a labourer if y'can 'elp it"). The Grammar School leavers generally got the clerical vacancies in local government, professional and railway offices, some to eventually leave the town when professionally qualified.

What is especially disappointing, even at this later hour, is the knowledge of what happened to several elementary school contemporaries. No early niche was available for their talents. Their later noteworthy careers — which in some cases did not begin until after war service — show the waste of those immediate post-school years.

Children born during the 1914/18 War or shortly before remembered little or nothing of those dreadful years. A vague recollection, possibly, of a khaki clad male apparently belonging to the household who suddenly arrived and, after a short while, left just as suddenly. Or of other khaki clad males who called spasmodically over a short period, brought one little presents, stayed to tea and finally walked off for the evening with a young aunt. And additionally perhaps, like me, retaining a blurred memory of waving a Union Jack at the town's victory parade.

Yet, with at most these few recollections, the war cast a long shadow over the full run of our 'Twenties childhood. At its outset, visual evidence in the persons of men minus a limb, less obviously an undue number of fatherless families. When these overt traces lost edge through familiarity, school kept war consciousness green. The Big Room's war memorial; also there, an artist's reconstruction of the Jutland deed that won young John Cornwell his VC; the annual Armistice Day ritual. Reminiscent talk of our elders too. Harrowingly, how a brave local lady, loser of three sons, was quite still and dry-eyed throughout the first emotional service after peace returned, even during the playing of the Last Post. Light heartedly recalling girls' flirtations with convalescent soldiers when our Drill Hall became their temporary home in 1917. And how one soldier in particular could hardly be forgotten because he had jilted, or was considered to have jilted, a young relative. How news of the Armistice reached the town and spread by word of mouth and an excited crowd converged on the Market Place like iron filings drawn by a magnet.

As time went on, transitory wartime courtships and the 11th of November 1918 faded from grown-ups' talk. But one aspect of the war cropped up with renewed life twenty years after the Armistice as another war loomed. It concerned those thought not to have "done their bit", who had not voluntarily enlisted and somehow evaded both the Derby Scheme and conscription. And of one who had been tardily roped in, achieved a commission, came through unscathed and tenaciously hung on to his military title for evermore. ("The bugger 'ed to be dragged in!")

Our two elders had long memories. So, assuredly, have my contemporaries. On a visit during the summer of 1976, I was told about a farm not far away where conscientious objectors were placed during 'our' war, an arrangement I had not heard of through overseas service and post-war exile. My informant recalled every inmate and laughingly told of the nickname locals had attached

Five Sail Mill,
Horncastle.

The Bull Ring,
Horncastle.

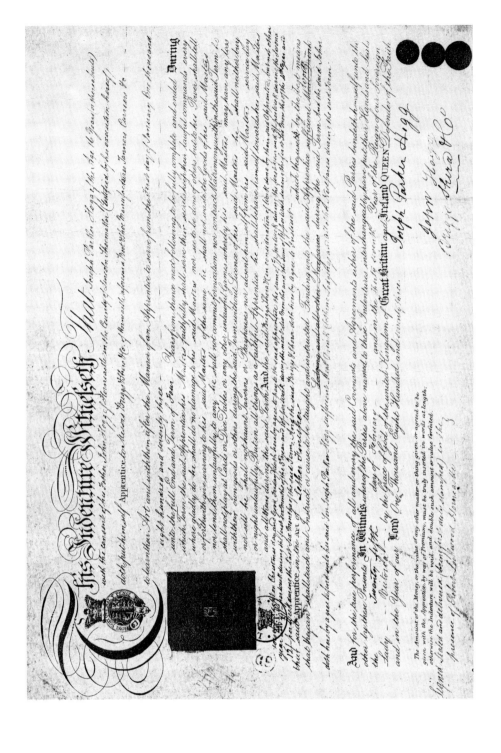

East Street, Horncastle.

to their domicile — Funk Farm. Unkind and unfair to genuine conscientious objection? Undoubtedly. But plain men often see matters as either black or white, and continue to do so even after the elapse of thirty years and more.

Unsurprisingly perhaps, national events generally touched us children very little. Neither did they appear to touch adult townspeople. The biggest 'Twenties upheaval', the General Strike, produced no local demonstrations, no struggles with policemen, but then it is highly unlikely the town possessed many trade unionists in 1926. (Gossip said one leading employer did not allow his men to join a union). So the 9-day Strike was chiefly memorable to me for the absence of our *Daily Chronicle* and the consequent deprivation of not being able to follow the exploits of the Australian cricket tourists.

The succession of aeronautical feats was a different matter. Lindbergh's epic Atlantic crossing in May 1927 really set alight an interest which Alan Cobham's long distance deeds had kindled over the previous two years. (The Alcock and Brown flight of 1919 came before newspaper and radio news had the power to engage our minds). And so we thrilled to the accomplishments of Bert Hinkler, Amelia Earheart, Kingsford Smith, Amy Johnson and others. These others included a leavening of high ranking ladies — the Duchess of Bedford, the Hon. Mrs. Victor Bruce and the ill-fated Hon. Miss Elsie Mackay who perished in an Atlantic attempt with her co-pilot, Captain Hinchcliffe. The RAF came much to our attention too, first with their flying boats and then, in 1929, their Schneider Trophy victory.

Modern Boy, a boys' weekly launched by the Amalgamated Press in the late 1920s, helped. It offered traditional fiction such as *Cloyne of Claverhouse*, about a schoolboy cricketing prodigy supposedly written, but more likely ghost

158

written, by Wally Hammond of Gloucestershire and England. But the paper's real purpose was the dissemination of information on exciting developments in aeronautics and other fields of mechanics. Especially racing cars. Boys' papers had given ample coverage to them from the opening of Brooklands in 1907, a coverage nicely complemented by silent films in which major stars (e.g. Wallace Reid) played. Now the spotlight frequently dwelt on solo attempts to establish new land speed records at Daytona Beach and elsewhere when two of the main contenders — Henry Segrave and Malcolm Campbell — were British. Fatal accidents that befell Parry Thomas in 1927 and Lee Bible, the day after Segrave's 231.363 m.p.h. in 1929, served to shape awareness of the dangers and drivers' courage. Segrave's own demise the following year, not in a car but an equally glamorous speedboat, blighted that June as if a friend had died.

Appalling also were the multiple deaths in the R101 disaster only a year after its 1929 launching, a disaster that effectively halted dirigible development. Airships had often figured in the more imaginative and futuristic fiction of *Boys' Magazine* and the D. C. Thomson quartet. *Boys' Magazine* was, so to speak, 'space minded', on one occasion giving 'free with every copy' tinted spectacles with which to view an eclipse of the sun. These spectacles consisted of a piece of white cardboard into which had been inserted two eye-size ovals of tinted celluloid-like material. Boys' weeklies could be topical: for example, *Pluck* ran a serial in 1924 with an Egyptology background following the opening of Tutankhamen's tomb.

A widely publicised event that did penetrate our consciousness was the 1924/25 British Empire Exhibition at Wembley. The penetration had a splendid start with the holding of the 1923 FA Cup final at the just-completed Wembley Stadium and the sensational happenings of an overspilling record crowd and the now legendary policeman on a white horse. Like the rest of the country, railway excursions to the Exhibition were organised. People returned with astonishing tales to tell — of the splendid pavilions and the marvels they contained — and souvenirs of booklets and programmes and brochures and cheap ornaments of metal and glass, all somewhere bearing the Exhibition's symbol of a squatting lion. Pavilions, printed matter and the rest took second place, however, with all children and a tidy percentage of adults to the huge amusement park. All the roundabouts, swings and side-shows of our experience were there in profusion plus a myriad never dreamt of. And, we could tell grown-ups who censored our movements, the amusement park had received the highest possible endorsement. Newspapers had prominently published a photograph of the King and Queen sampling the scenic railway. They sat facing each other on a coach's little seats, the King bowler-hatted with hands resting on the handle of his umbrella; Queen Mary, circular hat on piled hair, as always. Both still regal in spite of a very un-regal situation. No wonder they were popular, everybody said.

It is just possible to recall reasonably exactly how grown-ups spent their at-home evenings before the advent of wireless. One's first notion is that they spent them in talk. On going to bed when very young, apprehensive of darkness, I would ask for the stairfoot door to be left ajar so the reassuring hum of adult voices floated upwards to make a nightly lullaby, Often the voices were not only those from our household for there appeared to be an abundance of evening visitors, an abundance that included casual acquaintances besides intimates. Two aunts were still at home, young and unmarried. They were, like Grandma, active in Chapel affairs. People came from far and near to discuss choir and Sunday School arrangements, anniversary and Sale of Work tasks, harvest festival offerings. (Once Mr. Waymouth came just before my bedtime and was next day informed he would in due time be my teacher. A consequent feeling of depression is still remembered: schoolmasters had that effect then). People came to talk about secular pleasures too. Discussions on fancy dress dances — then popular functions — for instance, and, when costumes were decided, the preparations. The buying or begging of materials and paper patterns, buttons, hooks and eyes. Then my last sounds before falling asleep were young women's light talk and laughter interspersed with whirrings and squeaks from our treadled sewing machine. And I could sleepily visualise the scene as if actually present. Girls with pins in mouth corners, fingers busy with needle and thread, four or more sat round a table littered with open work baskets, little button tins, cotton reels, cloth remnants and sundry small feminine fripperies.

Having numerous visitors, both purposeful and casual, was typical of many households, I am sure. Our town tended to be garrulous. Of course there were the few who stated openly, or by action made plain, "They liked to keep themselves to themselves". An attitude respected but not really understood by an overwhelmingly convivial majority. ("There's nowt so queer as folk!"). So this overwhelming majority happily visited, the habit for many as haphazard as a cat wandering round a lengthy but known area. And the visited welcomed them all ("The more the merrier") and went on stitching, crocheting, embroidering, pegging hearthrugs and placing newly acquired picture post-cards in albums (to be disinterred, if Lincolnshire landscapes, generations later as fodder for local newspapers and county magazine), half of their minds on the flowing talk.

Less passively they sometimes sang songs round the piano. Years later a pile of dated popular music still bore witness to those singsongs. Selections from *Maid of the Mountains* and *Chu Chin Chow* and *The Bing Boys*, sheet music showing Marie Lloyd, Vesta Tilley and Talbot O'Farrell on the covers.

They must have got through a fair amount of reading too. One of my aunts in particular had a disposition towards self improvement, and to her the household owed its volumes of classics. And I discovered long afterwards in the back bedroom a neat pile of yellowing political/literary weeklies among the screened-off suitcases and baskets of apples, all from the heyday of Woodrow Wilson and Clemenceau and Edith Wharton. It made an interesting afternoon's browsing.

Strictly speaking, as 1921 was the first year, the Flood (*our* Flood) did not occur in the 'Twenties. A purely academic point, however, as its date was the 29th of May 1920 and the events of that day were talked about and milled over for the whole decade and more afterwards. Talk that received a fillip forty years on because of the second Flood in October 1960. After which then middle-aged or elderly residents dipped into fading recollections of the 1920 deluge to make comparison.

Personally, I can just remember the 1920 Flood. That it occurred on a Saturday, that I had never seen so much water (except at the seaside), of being carried in a grown-up's arms across a rushing stream that had replaced a cobbled roadway. There the recollection ends.

A latter-day account, based on reports of that celebrated Saturday, gives a full broad picture. The day started miserable and wet, hinting at eventual thunder but nothing worse. Rain continued to fall during the morning, though spasmodically. Then in the early afternoon, skies darkened. Great black clouds piled layer upon layer were menacing as an invading army. By two o'clock rain was tipling down as in a monsoon, rods of it that bounced up in miniature fountains on hitting pavement and cobblestone. But not for long. Town centre drains could not cope with the deluge. Streets nearest the rivers were soon submerged for those gentle pellucid streams had turned into broad, sweeping, brown torrents rising at least two feet an hour. An estimated six inches of rain fell in three hours.

The cause was a cloudburst over the Wolds to the north. A great head of water rushed down from the Wolds swamping inadequate river-beds at lower level. Our town, on its wedge of land betwixt rapidly swelling rivers, had no chance of escape. Streets submerged in earliest flooding were worst affected. In total, two hundred houses were flooded and an estimated (and then very considerable) £75,000 of damage done.

Eventually the waters receded leaving its legacy of thick oozy slime. The Primitive Chapel, sited on a fork joining two of the first streets to be flooded, suffered more than any other public building, water invading to a pew seat height. There was the inevitable crop of Flood stories just as twenty years later there were air-raid stories. Of how one West Street parlour got a four-inch covering in the time taken to re-stand a teapot. Of how in another water reached a height of three feet. More happily, how two doctors rescued a herd of cattle and of a woman who, with remarkable timing, had insured against flood only four days before. And of a renowned talking parrot, apparently swept away as it was never seen again.

Just as inevitably, came the post-mortem. Attention quickly focussed on the Stanch. Now the Stanch — a sluice to the south-west — was one of our town's best loved features. It was pleasant in fair weather to take a walk known as 'down the waterside' from the Wesleyan School along an ash strewn, river hugging path. That went through several kissing-gates (at points where hedges at right-angles to the river divided grassland into fields) to the Stanch, where water roared down beneath as you stood on its bridge. At the end of this May of 1920, nobody associated the Stanch with innocent pleasure but rather as the villain of the piece. For people contended that if the Stanch doors had been open damage would not have been anything like so severe.

They were probably right. In 1915 the Clerk of the Urban District Council set out in a letter to the Local Government Board the Stanch's position historically and factually, and voiced fears of possible disaster. A canal was constructed at the end of the eighteenth century, the water for which came from the larger river. The canal company erected the Stanch and a century later, around 1890, went out of existence and so the canal became derelict. The Urban Council subsequently carried out minor maintenance work but unfortunately a vital lock, a mile distant , was in the area of another authority. The gist of the Clerk's letter had been a request that his Council be given jurisdiction over the lock, the Local Government Board replied that it had no power to give such jurisdiction, nor could it express an opinion and merely advised the Clerk to take legal advice.

It was not possible, therefore, to apportion blame for this Act of God. But locals could count their blessings. No inhabitant had been drowned — Louth, to the north, had suffered greater devastation and 23 people had lost their lives.

A change from inter-war limited means to post-war's comparative affluence is accompanied by a change in ethos. The bedrock of native Lincolnshire kindness and so forth has not changed, but there is a perceptible shift — as everywhere else — in old attitudes. And, thanks to having the wherewithal, the ability to indulge new fads and fancies.

More rarely now do you get the incongruity of a modern dwelling completely stocked with old — as distinct from valuable antique — furniture. And in a diminishing number of small older houses, too, to find an unrelieved assemblage of old furniture. Not only can the occupants afford modern items but, as noted earlier, the most penny-wise young wives would cavil at having to make do with handed down sticks from previous generations. An example of a home stuffed with ancient furnishings was that of two octogenarian friends of my family. I called to see them after a lapse of many years and found their little terrace house, though bright, shining and spotless, hardly changed since I had first entered it half a century before. The living room still had the tall grandfather chair wedged between an aged drop-leaf table and the black-leaded kitchen range. A ceiling height built-in cupboard at the other side of the range appeared to more or less contain the same miscellany of crockery and cutlery and worn table linen that I remembered from all those years ago. In the parlour a huge picture of Mafeking being relieved still dominated one wall over a harmonium that had probably not been played for thirty years. None of the framed photographs adorning mantelpiece and circular table dated from later than the 1930s. All the chairs, including the larger fireside pair, were horsehair.

How big an interior contrast was presented by the house next door, lately occupied by young newly weds. Curtains, wallpaper, carpets and furniture seemingly straight from the advertisements of a glossy magazine. Gleaming fridge and washing machine in a recently added kitchen annexe, a handsome television set in the sitting room. A home, in short, three generations and more apart from my old friends'. "She goes out to work" and "Its all on h.p." they said. I replied mildly, hoping not to sound reproving, that this was now young folks' way. But my friends were not envious, just feeling wonderment at newfangled goings-on. Their generation — and mine too, for that matter —were brought up on the principle that, if you wanted something and couldn't afford it, you waited until you could. Hire purchase was deemed a snare for the feckless and an invention of the devil. It should be added my friends got on with their young neighbours extremely well, actually finding them refreshingly different. An example: the frequent clothes line exhibition of the girl's sketchy underwear causing them to wonder how she escaped pneumonia. The old people did not own a television set so had not seen the lingerie frequently displayed in dramas and commercial advertisements. Nor, apparently, did they notice boutique windows during their occasional visits to town.

As in every period, there were intimations in the decade's closing years of the next one, in this instance the very different 1930s. Different in that a Bright Young Things' ambience was irrelevant, impossible to carry forward because of early 'Thirties Depression and later 'Thirties gathering war clouds. The original Bright Young Things of circa 1922 were gettng a little long in the tooth, anyway, for dispensing this particular type of ambience.

Intimations were usually small, unobtrusive and not recognised as such. After all, one did not, and does not, be everlastingly on the look out for intimations and trends and portents. They are noticed (or more probably recalled afterwards) like a faint subtle scent. Minor things like changes in dance band instrumentation, for example. (Remember, we never *saw* professional bands perform in the flesh and rarely on film). In early days rhythm sections contained plonking banjos and grunting tubas and sousaphones. By 1929 guitars and double basses were substituted to give, with piano and drums, the basic rhythm section that lasted the remainder of the dance band era. Leading radio dance bands, those most sensitive barometers of transient popular musical taste, were illustrative of growing American influence. The dance band phenomenon originated in America. The best music for bands was composed by Americans — Gershwin, Berlin, Kern, Rodgers, Carmichael, Cole Porter and so on. It had a quality seldom approached by our native popular composers and has proved durable.

And the more obvious intimations. The way sleeker buses had completely supplanted the solid tyred, long box-on-wheels types of circa 1920, even giving a hint of later streamlining. That open char-a-bancs were becoming rarer. That postmen had exchanged helmets (which resmembled a Prussian soldier's minus the spike) for a glossy-peaked cap, presenting an appearance that remained unchanged for the next forty years.

But the overriding feeling was one of stability, of little or no change. In 1930 an acceptance of another war's inevitability lay several years ahead.

These, then, were the 'Twenties. Not to children growing up in a small East Midlands town noticeably the decade of Bright Young Things, Michael Arlen, smart brittle talk and P. G. Wodehouse slang. Besides a fact of geography these were also adult matters. The town did have echoes of them, one realises, but they were faint echoes. A noted lady killer known also as a drawing room ukelele strummer; local dance bands playing Gershwin; a small tight coterie of trend following middle-class young people.

And little else. No ripple from the aforementioned moderns among us disturbed the placidity of their seniors. For these seniors the old values — prudence and thrift and fair dealing and putting in a fair day's work —obtained as they had done from time immemorial. There were still the spoken and unspoken beliefs of knowing one's place, that the post-war tenet of Jack being as good as his master was, if true, true only up to a point. The majority of people concentrated on things they knew best: giving their labour without stint, getting the maximum crop from a cottage garden, making the money spin out.

A simple existence, obviously, far removed from the 'Twenties as experienced in Mayfair. But to us children it more than sufficed. The town was a good place to grow up in. I would have wished for an easier common lot but I, for one, would have changed the people not at all.